AN HOURGLAS

The Story of

JAMES A. FEEHAN

MERCIER PRESS

MERCIER PRESS
5 French Church Street, Cork
16 Hume Street, Dublin 2

Trade enquiries to CMD DISTRIBUTION,
55a Spruce Avenue, Stillorgan Industrial Park, Blackrock, Dublin

ISBN 1 85635 327 3
A CIP record for this book is available from the British Library.

10 9 8 7 6 5 4 3 2 1

Dedicated affectionately
to
my brother Seán Feehan
publisher, author and raconteur
who first encouraged me to write
and who lives on
in the Resurrecting Gift of Memory

Printed in Ireland by ColourBooks Ltd.

CONTENTS

ACKNOWLEDGEMENTS

I am indebted to Michelle Ivory for her long hours typing the manuscript, undaunted by her impending marriage. She even press-ganged her fiancé, Steve, into rushing copy to the publisher. As for John Derby, I cannot thank him enough for his efforts to make this book a reality. I owe him a great deal; I am grateful for the warmth of his friendship.

For permission to use copyrighted material, grateful acknowledgement is made to the following: Sinéad Ní Riain, for her brilliant photography; Father Bernie Hehir, editor of Wel-Com, *the New Zealand Catholic newspaper, for sending me pictures through the miracle of e-mail; Sister Kathleen and the estate of Andrew Finn, for the use of her father's poem on Ballinure; Diane and the estate of Sydney J. Watson, for drawing on her husband's research into the dalliance of a Protestant bishop's daughter and a future pope; Kathleen and the estate of Davy Cormack for the Derrynaflan verse; Father Godfrey Ainsworth, OFM, for his courtesy and kindness in permitting me to use his taped conversations with Sister Gertrude Joyce; Mary Guinan-Darmody of the Tipperary County Library, and Michael Dundon, editor of* The Tipperary Star, *for unearthing Pat McKenna's gem of Irish oratory.*

A special word of thanks to my friend Father Tom Fahey, who knew all the dramatis personae *in the story of the home-made earthquake, and to my friend and classmate Father Jerome Kiely, a gifted poet and writer, who read the manuscript and sent me back to the drawing board with his many helpful suggestions.*

INTRODUCTION

Reader, I have put into thy hands what has been the diversion of my idle and heavy hours.

John Locke (1632–1704)

The only possible excuse for this book is the year that's in it. The year 2000 is a jubilee year in more senses than one, because for me it marks fifty years spent as a priest: a priesthood that began in what were then the uttermost parts of the earth – Wellington, the capital of New Zealand – and is now in its twilight in Boherlahan, midway between Cashel and Holycross, a gem of a village in the crown of Tipperary.

The house where I am penning these memoirs is rather special, firstly because it was given as a gift to the parish by one of Boherlahan's most illustrious parishioners, Charles Bianconi, the 'King of the Irish Roads', and secondly because of its link with my origins. Often when I climb the five stone steps leading to the hall door I am reminded of a young man who mounted these same steps on 6 January 1908 to offer his services as a schoolteacher to the then parish priest, Father John Kelly. It was his first day ever in Tipperary, whither he was attracted from a teaching post in the Midlands by, of all things, the subtitle of a book. The book was Charles J. Kickham's classic *Knocknagow: The Homes of Tipperary.* Little did he realise, as he entered the first of the homes of Tipperary, that one day in the future one of his family would be living in this same residence. The young man about to be appointed principal of Ballytarsna School here in this parish was my father, Thomas Feehan.

Before long, my father would be making his own home here in Tipperary – and not, as it turned out, one home, but two. In 1915 he married Catherine O'Connor, also a schoolteacher in this parish. They lived in the teacher's residence in nearby Ballinree. Two children were born of this union: Seán in 1916 and Gerald in 1918. Gerald died in infancy and his mother passed away less then a year later.

In 1923 Thomas Feehan married Ellen O'Brien, who ran a small shop and post office in Ballinure, less than three miles from the school where he taught. He and Seán now made their home in Ballinure, and here two sons were born: myself in 1924 and Thomas (Jr) in 1928. Growing up, we had the rare good fortune of having two homes: the teacher's residence in Ballinree, where we sometimes spent the summer months, and the family homestead in Ballinure. I am the sole survivor of my father's two marriages.

These biographical data are intended as a backdrop to the sometimes personal nature of what follows. This book is, in the main, a sequel to two earlier works: *Stories for Preachers* and *Preaching in Stories*. The titles of these two books are self-explanatory. The Greek philosopher Aristotle in his classic work *Rhetoric* laid down what many regard as the basic model of communication: the speaker, the message and the audience. The Church adopted this model and called it: the preacher, God's message and the congregation. In our own times – and particularly in the wake of the communications revolution, with the new dimension of stories and the fresh emphasis on the whole network of human experiences – the preacher has to deal with three sets of experiences in getting the message across Sunday after Sunday: his own, the ones of Jesus and those of his listeners. In the new homiletics, the original model now becomes the story of the preacher, the story of God and the story of the listener. This, then, is in a sense the final part of a trilogy.

The book's title is from a poem by John Clare (1793–1864): 'What is life? An hourglass on the run!' For well nigh half a century I have tried to tell the story of God, in the hope that I might strike a responsive chord in the hearts of those listening to me. I have listened to people's stories of love and aversion, joy and sorrow, hope and disappointment, pleasure and pain, so much so that I am increasingly discovering that the golden years bring with them a flood of memories from the annals of the past and I feel an irresistible urge to jot them down before the sands of time finally run out. I am a writer in a hurry – an hourglass on the run!

The golden years have also brought with them an ever-increasing awareness that what I am determines the kind of message my hearers receive. A survey carried out by the Irish Liturgical Commission shows that what the majority of young people want to hear in the homily is the preacher's own story of faith. They expect the priest to give credible witness during the week to what he preached on Sunday. With good reason, because only too often the pulpit has been used as a platform for clerical idiosyncrasies and personal hang-ups – so much so that in many instances the story of God has gone untold. As a case in point, a pastor in my native parish was wont to unleash grim forebodings such as, 'If I were to lift the hob of hell I'd find a man from this parish stuck to the top of it!'

'Father,' a lady once said to a priest, 'your sermons terrify me, but your conduct consoles me!' Hence the relevance of the story of the preacher. Talking about our own grace experiences comes as a culture shock to many in my generation, as we were told in our seminary days to avoid personal references in our preaching, or anything that savoured of narcissism or navel-gazing.

The preacher who has himself been bruised by life can heal not from strength but from defeat. This is the theme of Henri Nouwen's book *The Wounded Healer.* The preacher who is himself a wounded healer brings an extra dimension of authenticity to his service and indeed to the telling of his story. There was a period in my life back in the 1970s when I went through a veritable dark night of the soul, stressed out by worry, fear and anxiety – and never more so than during those sleepless nights in Thurles Presbytery. The darkness that enveloped me was remorselessly punctuated by the cathedral clock tolling every quarter of an hour all through the night. I was wallowing in self-pity for my troubles, real and imaginary, and my ministry suffered as a result. Home and hospital visitation, even the confessional, became chores to be fulfilled merely out of a sense of duty.

The first glimmer of deliverance came in reading an article by Bishop Blougram, the Anglican Divine, in which he compared our life on earth to a chessboard made up of black and white squares. The white squares are the happy times, when the sun is forever shining and love, joy and peace reign in our lives. The black squares are when we find ourselves in a tunnel of darkness suffering from stress from whatever source: enveloping depression, bereavement, illness, anxiety – the litany is endless.

I dug out a chessboard that had been gathering dust for years and discovered that I had been moving with greater facility, and indeed relish, on the black squares of life than on the white ones. Carrying the analogy a step further, I found that each time I was on a black square – which was virtually all the time – I was touched on all sides by a white square: from above, from the sides and from below. Of course the converse was equally true but my main concern was to get out of the morass in which I was floundering.

One morning as I was reading the thirty-fourth psalm in my breviary, I discovered the first white square. The words leapt out at me: I sought the Lord and he answered me; from all my distress he set me free. The trouble is, we don't seek out the Lord that much in our secularised society. We tend to push him more and more into ever-shrinking corners of our lives. We ask: Is it any use seeking God today? Is he near enough? Can a God sitting on his deckchair above the clouds while the world suffers ... while you suffer ... while I suffer ... can that God handle our complex situations? Can he free me from my distress? The word 'seek' implies that I must make the first move on the chessboard: upwards, onto the white square above me. And the God that I found there was not an artificial creation but rather the stressed-out God of Gethsemane, who knows all about mental anguish, rejection, abandonment, loneliness and all the other ills that flesh is heir to. In the psalm, he was saying to me: I know what it's like. I've been through it all. Put your hand in mine and we'll see this thing through together. And, putting my hand in the hand of the man who stilled the waters, I found myself firmly entrenched on the first white square.

The next three moves were easy. To the left and right were family and friends. On these squares I found that a problem shared was a problem halved and that, by turning sacrifice into service, my own loneliness and depression were swallowed up in dispelling those of others. But it was on the fourth white square, the bottom one, that full and final deliverance awaited me, in the form of a ditty and an allegory. The ditty is a simple stanza by an unknown author:

Two books he read with great affection
The Gospels and a joke collection
And sang hosannas set to fiddles
And fed the sick on soup and riddles
So when the grave rebuke the merry
Let them remember Philip Neri
1515 to 95
Who was the merriest man alive
Then dying at eighty or a bit
Became a saint by holy wit

The allegory too is a lovely story about St Philip Neri. When he was an old man, a young priest came to Philip and asked him about the stages he had passed through in his quest for holiness.

'First, I found myself in the Land of Action,' said Philip. 'The day was not long enough to do all the things I wanted to do. Then God came to me and took me by the hand and led me into the Land of Sorrow. There I experienced the purifying effect of suffering and found myself in a new relationship with the divine. This led me into the Land of Love, where the last traces of self disappeared. This brought me to the Land of Silence, where I discovered contemplation.'

'And that was the end of your journey?' the young priest asked.

'No,' said Philip. 'God came to me again. He took me by the hand and said, "Today I am bringing you to the inner sanctuary, to the heart of God himself." And I was led to the Land of Laughter.'

The small measure of sanity that was left in me after my dark night of the soul I brought with me to be revived and refreshed in the Land of Laughter, thanks to Philip Neri. It was thanks to another Philip – this time the apostle Philip – that I was able to go on my way rejoicing.

The story is told in the Acts of the Apostles (chapter 8, verses 26–40) of how an angel of the Lord told Philip to go down the road leading south from Jerusalem to Gaza. There Philip met a high-ranking Ethiopian – the Minister for Finance – in the Court of Queen Candace, who was returning from Jerusalem, where the Ethiopian had gone to worship. The Ethiopian was in his chariot reading the fifty-third chapter of the prophet Isaiah, 'The Song of the Suffering Servant', when Philip joined him and, beginning with this chapter, showed him who Jesus was. When the man became a believer the apostle baptised him at the next watering spot on the route south. Now, baptism by immersion, which was the practice for adults in the early Church, symbolised two things: cleansing from sin and being flooded with the Grace of Christ – a real union with Christ. As the waters closed over a person's head he seemed to die with Christ, and as he emerged he rose with Christ, a new man to a new life (Romans 6:1–4). Then we are told that Philip disappeared and, in a lovely phrase, that the Ethiopian went on his way rejoicing. Tradition has it that the Ethiopian went home and evangelised his own country. Whether or not this is true, we can be sure that he would not have been able to keep his new-found joy to himself.

The following pages abound with stories of people –

many of them my colleagues in the priesthood – who could not keep their joy to themselves. As I write, three of them are waving for attention: the priest who preached at his own funeral, another who created an earthquake that shook the west coast of New Zealand's South Island (with tremors of laughter) and, finally, my cherished colleague and classmate who one evening sat by the side of the road drinking tea out of a tin mug with the travelling people and the following evening sat down to tea with the Queen of England, later describing his hostess as a 'grand little shtump of a woman, very aisy to talk to'. Sounds incredible! But bear with me, gentle reader, and read on.

These are just some of the characters in this book who were laughed at and loved, mimicked and mourned – who brought joy and sunshine into my life and sent me on my way rejoicing.

JAMES A. FEEHAN
Boherlahan
18 June 2000

1

The Big House

The memories really begin in Ballinure, the village in south Tipperary where I was born and raised. The cross was the focal point of the village: it was the axis around which our lives revolved, our exit to the outside world and the forum where men gathered in the evenings to discuss politics and horses, the price of cattle and pigs, the weather and the crops. They gathered at Din Dwyer's frontage and across from them on the windowsill of Bulfin's sat three patriarchal figures: Mickey Bulfin; George Tutty, who was coachman at the big house, and Joe Max, the local blacksmith. They were known as the Upper House. Whilst the adults engaged in their deliberations, we children played handball against the smooth surface of Mike Dwyer's store or skittles on the nearby plain patch; here also we played marbles and spun our tops and vied with one another in collecting the registration numbers of passing cars, which, needless to say, were few and far between.

Outsiders who passed through the cross on their bicycles were sometimes subjected to derisive comments and, in the case of ladies, good-natured banter, usually emanating from Jim Dwyer of the Buildings, who confessed to a 'strong wakeness' for the fair sex. One of Jim's prime targets was Maggie O'Sullivan, a prim, prissy and proper woman with a tiny little body who had her sights firmly focused on the religious life. Whenever she passed, she had to run the gauntlet of Jim's raillery, until one evening the moth-eaten

Romeo from the Buildings crossed a bridge too far and besought Maggie to give him a birdie (a kiss). Red as a beetroot, Maggie dismounted her bicycle, strode over to her tormentor and, in the presence of the assembly, administered a solemn warning, punctuated by an admonishing finger rhythmically tapping the saddle of her bike: 'Jim Dwyer! Now I'm warning you! In future don't mix, meddle or make with me! Because if you do, you will know the consequences!'

She then took her case to the triumvirate in session on Mickey Bulfin's windowsill. As she narrated the story of her humiliation, the three nodded their heads sagely and unanimously agreed that Dwyer's overtures to an aspiring nun were out of order and, in George Tutty's words, 'totally indecorous'. Joe Max delivered the judgement of the Upper House to the Buildings' Casanova and, from that evening until she entered the convent shortly afterwards, Maggie had untrammelled and harassment-free transit through the cross of Ballinure.

After a lifetime of teaching in George's Hill Convent in Dublin's inner city, Maggie died recently in her hundred and third year. As I write, a rather whimsical image keeps crossing my mind of Maggie passing through the Pearly Gates to receive the reward, which the Lord promised to those who leave all things to follow him, only to find herself being propositioned once more by Jim Dwyer for that elusive birdie! Can't you just see her flouncing past him, wagging that rebuking finger: 'For the course of eternity, don't you mix, meddle or make with me, *Saint James!'*

Marring the idyllic vista of Ballinure cross is the demesne wall, which stretches for miles and lines two of the four roads that meet at the intersection. It was the longest structure of its kind in the parish – a long wall built by the gentry to keep themselves in and the tenantry and peasantry out. The wall, which was straight across from our house, will be forever etched in my memories of childhood. We had to go upstairs to peer over the wall at the big house set in beautiful woodland and surrounded by 2,000 acres of the richest pastureland in Tipperary. The Noan estate, as it was called, was the property of Frederick Rhodes Armitage. Like many such estates, it was originally given to an officer in Cromwell's army, Nathaniel Taylor, and it remained with the Taylors before passing on to the Armitages in 1860.

Freddy Armitage succeeded his father, Dr Thomas Rhodes Armitage, in 1902. He became high sheriff of County Tipperary in 1906. He owned virtually every house in Ballinure until land-purchase legislation compelled him to sell out to his tenants in 1922. One of the beneficiaries of this arrangement was my mother, who had a two-storey house which included a shop, a post office and an adjoining garden.

The iniquitous wall was the dividing line. Not alone did it cut us off from the lush green pastures and woodlands of Noan, but it effectively divided us from our 'betters'. These people felt themselves to be not merely from a different class to us but also of a different race, religion and lifestyle, and they took their political philosophy from England. They had two sons and three daughters. The sons would have inherited the estate, but when the Second World War broke out Stanley and Benny felt duty-bound to enlist in the British forces, where a cruel fate awaited them. Benny was a lieutenant aboard the *Prince of Wales* when it was torpedoed and sunk by the Japanese on 10 December 1941. All on board the ship were killed. Two years later Stanley was captured, tortured and killed in a prisoner-of-war camp in the East Indies.

To add to Freddie's grief, his wife, Ellen, was killed in a road accident on her way to Dublin on 17 February 1942. He himself died in 1952, having left the property to his daughter Doris. With her passing in 1979, the Armitage link with Noan was broken, and with it the passing of an era.

One abiding memory that I have carried with me since childhood is seeing the Armitage ladies, Doris and Eleanor, riding into our yard every afternoon to post their mail and purchase bread, which had to be fresh: today's bread today. On one such occasion, the shop was full, it being pension day, and Jim Lar, one of the local characters, was regaling us with a story which had just a trace of vulgarity – enough to send him into a spasm of raucous laughter. The mirth, however, ceased abruptly when he realised that the genteel ladies from Noan were already on the premises, having heard every word of the vulgar narrative. Jim was profuse in his apologies, doffing his cap obsequiously first to Doris and then to Eleanor. 'Oh, its quite all right, James,' was the gracious response of Doris, 'your story was rather risqué, but quite hilarious'.

When the ladies left, my mother, assuming her most severe postmistress demeanour, glared at the penitent Jim Lar and said scathingly, 'Well indeed, all I can say is, the cheek and impertinence of the lower order makes the quality blush!'

Many of the big houses – and with them a large portion of Ireland's architectural heritage – were burned to the ground during the troubles. 'Any idiot with petrol and a match can set fire to a house,' commented Monk Gibbon. 'It needs trained architects, masons and carpenters to build a house. The latter class of technical competence is rare, the former are numerous.'

'The British loyalists were paying dearly, the demesne walls were tumbling,' wrote Tom Barry. 'Our only fear was that, as time went on, there would be no more loyalist homes to destroy'. Noan escaped destruction, but only just. When the IRA took away the chauffeur at the big house, Dave Cummins – a known loyalist who returned to his native Belfast every year to celebrate the Twelfth – and shot him in Dualla on suspicion of giving information to the RIC, Freddy Armitage decided to take his wife and all his family to England until the troubles were over. When he returned, he found that a large amount of furniture had been stolen from the house and numerous trees had been felled during his absence.

Frank McCan, nephew of Pierce McCan, patriot, TD and president of the Tipperary IRA, told me that when the news of his uncle's death in Gloucester Prison broke, one of the first to call to Ballyowen to offer their condolences were Freddy Armitage and his wife.

The school in Ballinure was built in 1843 at a cost of £60 by the Noan estate and affiliated to the Board of Education in 1844. It was situated opposite the demesne wall, about half a mile from the village, and was called Noan National School. It consisted of just one room. When I enrolled there in 1927, there were no toilets or playgrounds. The lack of toilets was overcome by having recourse to bushes and hedges in adjoining fields. Once a year the steward from the big house brought down to the school a box of egg sandwiches. This was our annual treat. Needless to say, this dreadful construction was closed in the 1940s and replaced by the present school.

The basic elements of education in those days were a boy, a book and a stick, and the book, particularly the catechism, was beaten into the boy with the stick. My dominant memory of this school was the cruelty and brutality of the regime. My younger brother, Thomas, was literally beaten black and blue when he was just eight years old. I am still haunted by the memory of the marks on his body and the delirium and dysfunctional effects of the thrashing that he suffered; these things were to last throughout his life. My father was loath even to make a complaint against a teacher colleague, so no further action was taken. The *personae* in this drama are all, including Thomas, long since departed to a better land, I hope and pray.

'No one shouted stop!' These words belong to John Healy and a series of articles he wrote for the *Irish Times* in October 1967. At the time, they were hailed as some of the finest pieces of social comment published by an Irish newspaper in over half a century. In one of the most scathing of these articles, Healy spoke of the sad history of education in his native village. He could have been speaking about Ballinure. We had a rat-infested school built in the middle of the nineteenth century. From it to the nuns and brothers and the technical schools – six and a half miles away in Cashel and eight and a half miles away in Thurles – went the lucky few who could afford a secondary education. If your people had money, you got a secondary education; if they didn't, you went without. Then, in 1967, along came Donogh O'Malley and his free post-primary education for all, with buses to pick the pupils up in the morning and ferry them home again in the afternoon. Healy recalls his mother saying, 'If O'Malley has the blessings of every mother in this parish, he has earned it. Isn't it a great thing besides long 'go, when they had to scrape and save and even then most of them couldn't think of sending one away.'

Wasn't is a great thing besides 'long 'go'! If there was one family that had good reason never to forget 'long 'go', it was that of Tom and Mary Higgins of Cooleagh. They and their ten children eked out an existence on just over three acres of marshy land on the fringe of the Bog of Allen. O'Malley's munificence came, alas, too late for the Higginses.

My father used often recall the day the Higginses came to his school in Ballytarsna. All of nine of them walked across the bog, on transfer from the Ballinure academy. He had good reason to remember them, because only a few weeks previously he had been cycling to Ballinure to post some letters and, as he'd passed the Higgins homestead, they had taken off after him, boys and girls, and pelted him with missiles – pieces of peat and rotten apples – all the way to the Ballinure creamery. Needless to say, he took a more circuitous route to Balinure after that! He recalled how the face of Paddy Higgins, the leader of the ambush, fell when he recognised 'the Master', as he was to be affectionately known to them from that day onward.

'Higgins, how many of you are there? Give me your names also,' my father asked.

'Well, sir,' said Paddy, after a quick survey of his siblings, 'there's meself, that's wan, and there's Jack and Chris and Jimmy, that's how many ... that's four,' he continued, ticking them off on his fingers. 'Then there's the three girls, Ciss, Katty, and Lizzy. That's ...' Again he silently computed. 'That's seven! That only laves Mick and Dan. Isn't that nine, sir?'

'It is, Higgins,' my father replied. 'You're quite good at the sums, but you're a pretty poor marksman! So now, no more ballistics on the Cooleagh Road. Is that a deal?'

'Oh it is, sir,' said Paddy, wondering what ballistics meant, and then adding, with a grin, 'as well as the nine of us here, we have another on the road.' He was referring to the youngest sibling, who was later to be called Tone (short for Anthony) but was as yet just another worried look on his father's face.

My father always maintained that the Higgins pupils had a higher IQ than the average family in the school and that it was a sin crying out to heaven for vengeance that they were denied the education that would lift them out of the poverty trap. He used rage at the inactivity, for close on fifty years, of self-government, especially when he saw Paddy Higgins at election time canvassing for the politicians who denied him and his family the education which was their basic human right.

They could have taken the train at Laffansbridge that would bring them to the nearest boat to England armed only with the rote questions and answers of the Butler *Catechism*, a set of rosary beads in their pocket and little else. But the Higginses were a proud clan, deeply attached to their family, to one another and to their homeland. Not one of them ever emigrated. Only three of them married, and now there is not one of them left. Those of us left behind can only sigh and wonder for what might have been, had only

Donogh O'Malley appeared on the scene a bit earlier.

No picture of our village would be complete without a visit to the forge. Apart from the cross of Ballinure and the creamery, the remaining forum for discussion of politics, horses, hurling matches and the harvest was Joe Max's forge. Joe was a patriarchal figure with a long white beard, and it was often a cause for wonder that his beard did not catch fire when the huge bellows sent sparks dancing all over the place. Pictures and memories keep coming to me through the arches of the years of Joe's forge and its surroundings. The great black walls, hung here and there with horseshoes and all kinds of rusty ironwork; the deep night of its recesses that was only lightened by the ruddy blaze from the great fire; the horses coming in, some terrified, some submitting quietly to the operation of being shod, Joe lifting up the hoof into his leather apron, the smell of burnt cartilage, the 'tap, tap' of the hammer, the quivering of the poor animals, but most of all the metallic music that echoed all day from the anvil.

Only recently on a visit to Prague, I saw Verdi's opera *Il Trovatore,* and when it came to the mighty 'Anvil' chorus, I closed my eyes and pictured Joe Max up there on the stage beating time on his anvil to Verdi's music.

Freddy Armitage and the ladies from the big house came to Joe to have their horses shod. When the ladies came into the forge, there would be a hush to the conversation. Joe would deferentially doff his cap, as would all his clientele. Sometimes, Harold Clarke, a regular visitor to the forge, would bring along the Armitage horses. Harold was our local barber. He lived in the gate lodge at the entrance to the big house and, in keeping with his status, referred to himself as a tonsorial artist. He was as deaf as a stone but was so gifted as a lip-reader that he could complete sentences almost as soon as they were begun.

My brother Seán, another regular visitor to Joe's forge, was privileged to be numbered amongst Joe's bellow-blowers until the infuriated blacksmith abruptly dispensed with his services. One afternoon, as Joe was diligently engaged in his craft, Seán took a sticky substance which he had for catching birds (he freed them later, it must be added) and spread it over the nails that were used in the shoeing process. When the time came to hammer home the nails in the horse's new footwear, they stuck to Joe's fingers, rendering the operation impossible. The culprit ran for his life, pursued by Joe, brandishing his tongs and screaming, 'The curse of God on you, Jack Feehan!'

Growing up in a country post office was, in retrospect, a rather unusual experience, deserving of a mention in these memoirs. My mother inherited the role of postmistress from her aunt, who took her in as her assistant when she was just seventeen. Her first week's wages amounted to one shilling, which she wrapped in brown paper and took to Killenaule, four and a half miles away, to deposit in a post office account. 'I walked back to Ballinure,' she later recalled, 'with my head in the air. Now I was a lady of means!'

The post office put us in contact with the entire community. They all came to us to purchase stamps and seldom left without buying something in the shop. This was good for business and helped us keep pace with the village's bigger store, which was owned by Mike Dwyer, with whom we had the most cordial relations. This was especially true during the war years, when commodities were hard to come by, so that if one shop was in short supply the other helped out. This was just another example of the *muintearas* which adorned rural life in those days.

On Fridays the elderly came for their old-age pension, which amounted to the princely sum of ten shillings a week. It was wonderful listening to them as they recreated memories of the past. These were moments to be cherished, and how I looked forward to them.

The mail arrived each morning at 9 am – by bicycle! I often think of the Thurles postmen making the eight-and-a-half mile journey from town, cycling in all kinds of weather, sometimes drenched to the skin; the trays in front of the handlebars laden with parcels; making deliveries en route and then facing a return journey back to Thurles with outgoing mail. All this for a pittance in wages!

Pake Kirwan, the local postman, was a member of every family and yet belonging to none except his own. On his daily rounds he would chat with virtually everyone he met, sitting on his bicycle with his feet firmly planted on the ground, a posture that I've never seen repeated. In trouble of any kind, and particularly in times of death or bereavement, he was the first on the doorstep to offer his condolences. Everything was left in Pake's hands. He made the funeral arrangements, dug our graves and buried our dead. In later years he lost his eyesight and could no longer travel out to mingle with the people he knew so well. His days were spent in the kitchen, thumbing his beads in the loving care of his wife, Nance. Pake had surely a host of friends awaiting him when the Lord beckoned him home to the Eternal Vision.

And finally there was Willie Duggan, who was in all our eyes 'the noblest Roman of them all'. Willie brought postal deliveries into the twentieth century when he arrived in Ballinure in the green postal-service van. His smiling countenance, sparkling wit and stores of stories enriched all our lives. Bringing up a large family on meagre wages in difficult times, he was determined that his children would have what he had never had. That's how he explained to me his decision to take on an evening job after an arduous day of routine work. He became my parishioner when I was appointed to Thurles, and in my frequent visits to his home I witnessed first-hand his total dedication and commitment to Bridie and the children in his role as husband and father.

When my parents got on in years and were unable to travel to the parish church, four and a half miles away, for Sunday Mass, Willie would drive out Sunday after Sunday and take them to Mass in Thurles cathedral so that afterwards they could spend some time with me. Then he would take them back home. Death came to Willie at a relatively early age, but not before his family were able to repay him one-hundredfold for the sacrifices he had made for them. He and Bridie were brought to the United States, England, the French Riviera and other exotic places that until then they could only dream about.

Before he died I reminded him of his kindness to my own parents, but with characteristic modesty he brushed the compliment aside with an 'Ah sure, why wouldn't I?'

I pursued the subject by recalling the Lord's own words to the effect that any one who gave even a cup of cold water to a disciple in his name would not lose his reward. 'Willie,'

I said, 'what you gave to my parents was not just a cup of cold water, it was sheer sparkling champagne. Can't you just imagine what he has in store for you?'

Willie just smiled and gripped my hand. Words were not necessary. Shortly afterwards he heard the only words that really matter: 'Well done, good and faithful servant!'

2

FARMING – A BAD BUSINESS

One Friday afternoon in the closing stages of the Second World War, a group of old-age pensioners were in the shop, drawing their meagre ten shillings a week. It was a time of severe food rationing, which included one half-ounce of tea per person per week, and farming was, in the words of one of those present, a bad business. The conversation was about the sad state of the country, when John Fogarty entered the shop. John was a brilliant student, later to become a university professor and dean of the Faculty of Arts in UCC. He had with him a newspaper giving all the lurid details of the atomic bombs that had been dropped on the Japanese cities of Hiroshima and Nagasaki. He was trying to explain the concept of the bomb to the farmers present when one of them interjected, 'Well, John, I remember the economic war of the 1930s, but this economic bum must be the divil entirely!'

The atom and the nuclear explosions were beyond the comprehension of the farmer but the devastation they caused was enough to evoke memories of a farming community struggling for survival as it found itself stoically staggering through the economic war of the 1930s and the privations of the Second World War in the next decade. It was a difficult time for farmers; cattle prices were rock-bottom. I can recall my father buying two Kerry cows from a Kilkenny farmer for a total of £12.

Times were harder still for farm labourers. They eked

out a miserable existence, with some of them trying to raise large families on five shillings a week. Paddy O'Donnell, a lifelong and cherished friend of mine, started as a farm labourer on leaving school and, needless to say, worked for a pittance. When the farm began to prosper, he asked his employer for a raise but was turned down. Paddy now takes up the story. 'I bided my time until the first of May, when I got up early while the rest of them were asleep. I took half a dozen eggs out of the hen house and broke them on the farmer's crops. There was a *piseog* at the time that to break eggs in such a manner on May Day was sure to bring a curse on the crops.

'Things rested so,' continued Paddy, 'until we were at dinner that same day, when one of the sons rushed in in a panic, telling his father to come quick and see the curse that had been wreaked on the crops. Then I was sent to the parish priest to tell him to come straight away and bless the crops. Now, mind you, I felt a bit quare going on such a mission, seeing that 'twas I brought the curse on in the first place. But go I did, and the parish priest came and scattered holy water where I had broken the eggs.

'But there was even better to come,' he added, with a mischievous grin. 'The parish priest came and said Mass in the house on the following day and I, the culprit, was asked to serve the Mass. And serve the Mass I did the next day, and the priest said special prayers for the farmer and his crops. He reminded the Lord of what a good Catholic my employer was and that he was a pillar of the Church, so he was. And all the time I was secretly praying that the curse would work and I kept telling the Lord what a scoundrel the so-and-so was.

'After the Mass the priest had a fine breakfast in the parlour of rashers, eggs and puddings – black and white – while I had to make do in the kitchen with a mug of tay and a thick slice of bread, and you should have seen the way the farmer's wife scraped the butter on to it. I never found out which won, the curse or the blessing, because I was off to England the following week. And do you know, Jimmy, England was the making of me. I got a steady job, was well paid and then came home and married my childhood sweetheart, Statia. All the family did well, thanks be to God, which is more than can be said of the crawthumper's brood. So maybe,' he concluded, with a grin, 'the eggs did their job after all.'

A couple of years ago I officiated at Paddy's funeral Mass. There were tears in my eyes as I preached the homily but they soon turned to smiles when the gifts were brought up in the Offertory procession. As well as the bread and wine and other items betokening Paddy, on a small tray carried by one of his sons were four eggs! He smiled as he handed them over. I smiled too and I am sure that the Man Above must have smiled as well when he heard the story from Paddy.

The harvest was the main source of livelihood; reaping it was a laborious process which called for sharing and willing hands; saving it depended on the weather. The reaping hook was the basic implement for centuries. It was slow work made light by willing hands. The scythe replaced it, halving the harvest as it cut meadows and oatfields in half the time. But again, many scythes brought quicker results.

Then along came the horse-drawn mowing machine,

which reduced the manpower required even further. Denis O'Sullivan and his horse would team with Son Bulfin and his horse and the two mowing machines in one half-day would do what would take a troupe of scythes two days to accomplish.

Farm technology reached its zenith, or so we thought, when the first tractor came to the village and did in an hour what it took two men and a pair of horses half a day to do. It cut out Denis O'Sullivan and his horse pairing up with Son Bulfin and his horse for the spring ploughing and the summer hay-cutting. It cut out the line of carts drawing turf from the bog and the trolleys bringing trams of hay to the hayshed.

And in the autumn the pervasive tractor, with yet another accessory, made ominous inroads into the last remaining community event in farming – the threshing. It replaced the steam engine. The automated sound of the combine would replace the rhythmic hum of the threshing mill and in so doing sound the death knell of *muintereas,* or neighbourliness, as we knew it. Long before the advent of television, and how we worried over its Anglo-American values, another and earlier technology had already altered the cultural patterns of rural Ireland, and we never recognised it or what it was doing to our people.

One man who lived and laboured through all this changing technology was my neighbour and friend since childhood, Tom Bulfin. Just a few hours before he died, he opened his eyes and saw me standing at the foot of the bed. He smiled and sighed, 'Weren't they grand, father – the auld times.'

What a poignant exit line! Only Denis O'Sullivan and

Jack Nolan now remain of Tom's contemporaries. The rest have vanished like the snows of yesteryear.

A boon blessing for small farmers and labourers with a yearning for their own bit of land was the division of large estates. The first one to be divided in our community was the Myers Estate in Grallagh, which comprised 1,100 acres. This changed the entire scenario, as former labourers became farmers overnight. Those fortunate to receive allotments were invited to Dublin to sign the necessary documentation at the Land Commission. Travel expenses were paid and they were invited to lunch at the Ormonde Hotel on the quays. Amongst the beneficiaries of this largesse was Jack Power, who regaled the village shoppers the next day with his experiences in the metropolis.

'The grandest people I ever met', was how he described the civil servants in the Land Commission, and as for the lunch in the Ormonde, he just ran out of superlatives. 'We had lashings and leavens of everything,' he declared. 'Soup I thank you, every kind of mate, and as for the puddings afterwards, I never ate the like of them.'

'Tell me Jack,' said my mother, with a mischievous glint, 'did ye get any napkins?'

'Napkins, Mrs Feehan,' he retorted. 'I declare to God, sure I ate plates of them.'

It was a common sight in the days before electricity and fridge-freezers to see flitches of bacon hanging from hooks on the kitchen ceiling of every farmer's house in Ballinure and its environs. Depending on the size of the household, a pig would normally be killed twice a year. The sacrificial altar was a dray cart lifted off its axle and laid on the ground. Then, in another exercise in neighbourliness, two men would catch the pig; another had a rope with a loop, which would be put into the pig's mouth to keep it from biting. Then the misfortunate animal would be turned on its back and tied by the legs to the four corners of the cart.

Every neighbourhood had an expert in dispatching the pig but sometimes the services of a specialist were invoked. Harry Sheppard belonged to this elite corps of porcine executioners, and whenever his services were required the number of onlookers would increase significantly to see the maestro exercising his craft. No surgeon ever wielded his scalpel with the expertise with which Harry inserted his knife in the pig's throat. Instead of an anaesthetist and nurses, he would have women standing by to channel the blood into an enamel basin under the cart. The ladies would then take the basin of blood away to make black puddings.

Then Harry would begin the process of scalding the pig. The carcass would be placed on an iron gate lying flat and resting on blocks. Scalding water would be poured on it – hot enough to remove grit and hairs and ensure a clean cadaver. Superflua, like the heart, liver and intestines, were removed, and even the bladder had its uses. It would be washed, disinfected and subsequently inflated and used as a football by the children. The meat would then be cut into fairly large flitches, salted, barrelled and, after three weeks, hung on hooks in the kitchen ceiling. Delicacies like the griskins (pork-steaks) were eaten straight away or shared with the neighbours. The smoked bacon would ensure a meat supply for six months.

Harry Sheppard was a master of many arts and crafts.

Besides his expertise in dispatching and dissecting pigs, he was also much in demand as a thatcher and repairer of farm machinery. In the lore of his native Barraderragh, he could turn his hand to almost anything, with one notable exception: he never milked a cow! He would skilfully parry any queries about this apparent blemish on his otherwise impressive *curriculum vitae* by declaring, 'Who'd want to milk a cow with six women in the house?' Shades of chauvinism, perhaps!

A Protestant by birth, Harry showed little interest in Catholicism until he met the winsome Margaret Ryan from neighbouring Aughnagomaun, who was to win his heart and hand. As the romance developed, the issue of religion inevitably came to the fore and, as Harry felt ill at ease about approaching a priest, he did the next best thing in the context of the times – he went to the local schoolmaster, who happened to be my father, Thomas Feehan. I am being unashamedly biased when I assert that my father was an outstanding teacher of religion; that I learned more basic theology from him that I ever absorbed in the lecture halls of Maynooth. In Harry he found an enquiring mind, and he often had to delve into his back-up resources to deal with the young man's probing questions. When the course was completed, my father went with Harry to see the parish priest, who was amazed at Harry's grasp and knowledge of the faith. His reception into the Church was a mere formality.

Harry's newly acquired knowledge of the Catholic faith stood to him in great stead on one occasion, when he was having a religious discussion with a local farmer. By all accounts, Harry was getting the better of the argument when the other resorted to the cheap jibe, 'Of course, you are only a convert and wouldn't know much about these issues.'

'You've hit the nail on the head,' was Harry's rejoinder. 'You see the difference between the two of us is, I became a Catholic with my intelligence, whereas you didn't.'

Game, set and match to Harry!

3

Guards and Peelers

A recent visit to Ballinure conjured up visions of Goldsmith's *Deserted Village.* There are no more gatherings at the cross since the motor car widened the horizons and people began to go far afield for their pleasures. The Three Wise Men at Mickey Bulfin's windowsill have long since gone to God and, of the four corner houses on the cross, only two are now occupied. The *paterfamilias* of the community, Denis O'Sullivan, now in his nineties, recalling the troubles, told of Mickey Bulfin and his family having to get out of their house at three hours' notice to make way for over fifty Black and Tans who occupied the premises for four months. He remembers the Tans playing soccer at the crossroads. At the same time there were twenty RIC men in the barracks across the road. These are the two houses that are now empty.

Dualla, just over two miles away, was a hotbed of republicanism. The inspirational figure there in the struggle for freedom was Pierce McCan, who, as I mentioned earlier, was a TD and president of the Tipperary Brigade of the IRA. McCan was arrested by the RIC and the British army in Ballyowen and died in Gloucester Prison on 6 March 1919. Michael Collins was one of those who carried his coffin to Kingsbridge Station for a hero's welcome in Tipperary. He is buried in the republican plot in his native Dualla with two Ballinure brothers shot by the British forces – James and Lawrence Looby of Grallagh – together with Patrick Hogan and William Delaney, who were killed in action in the War of Independence.

The RIC were never forgiven for the role they played in the arrest of Pierce McCan and, until the civic guards replaced them in 1922, they were viewed with misgivings and suspicion. They were called Peelers, a disparaging reference to their origins. During his second term as Home Secretary, Sir Robert Peel (1788–1850), future British prime minister, established the Metropolitan Police, members of which were nicknamed Bobbies and Peelers after him.

It should be remembered, however, that the vast majority of the RIC, particularly in the rural areas, were amongst the finest young men that rural Ireland produced, at a time when there were scant opportunities. Few of the young country lads who joined the force even believed that they were representing an alien power. When the War of Independence took place, they were easy targets for violence and ambush. One member of the Ballinure constabulary was shot dead just a mile from the village on his way home from Cashel, where he had gone to collect his wages. In the aftermath of independence, many members of the RIC emigrated, some becoming part of police forces in Northern Ireland, Britain and the United States. Those who remained in Ireland kept quiet about their past, as did their families. They have no memorial, no cenotaph and no testimonial to their services. They are, in many respects, a lost generation of Irish manhood.

The first civic guards to arrive in Ballinure in 1922 – a sergeant and three guards – were not long in breaking down the barriers of suspicion and mistrust. They were unarmed and they wove their way into the fabric of daily life in this rural community by helping out at threshings, turf-cutting, hay-saving and every activity that brought the people together in a spirit of *muintearas*. They showed themselves to be protectors of those who were vulnerable; thus they became a social force – an influence in our midst for rightness.

What I am trying to say is best exemplified by an unforgettable experience at the Golden Jubilee celebrations of the Tipperary Garda Division in August 1972. The celebrations began with a special Mass in Thurles cathedral. Chief celebrant was Archbishop Thomas Morris, and he was joined by eight priests, all of them sons of serving or retired gardaí. After the impressive ceremony, a celebratory dinner was held in the Premier Hall, and of course there were the customary speeches by the Archbishop, Minister for Justice, Garda Commissioner and a few other VIPs.

But the highlight of the evening was a gem of Irish oratory by retired sergeant Pat McKenna of Thurles. He was replying to the toast to the guests. Who shall ever forget the ringing sincerity of his voice as its cadences resonated throughout the huge assembly, only to be punctuated by rounds of tumultuous applause? What follows is a précis of what he said on that memorable occasion.

> Last week, fifty years ago, we, the young boys of the newly formed civic guards, wore uniform for the first time in the streets of Dublin. It was a sad occasion at the funeral of Arthur Griffith; ten days afterwards, we wore the same uniform for the second time – this week fifty years ago on a very tragic occasion, when we marched at the funeral of Michael Collins. Those two great men spearheaded the executive conference for the formation of the civic guard, the name under which it was then known. It was unanimously decided that we would be unarmed.
>
> After seven months' training at various centres in Dublin

and Kildare, the next month – 25 September 1922, to be exact – we (there are twenty-five of us here present tonight) went out in small groups and manned the principal barracks in the cities and larger towns of Ireland. Our recent hard-won freedom was conceived in violence and born into an atmosphere of hatred, suspicion and brotherly distrust. Brave men – comrades who had stood shoulder to shoulder in the four glorious years in the struggle for independence – became bitter enemies in a bloody civil war.

In that atmosphere and in those circumstances, we, the young boys of the civic guard, looked upon as the cream of Irish manhood, went out to the country to establish and maintain law and order and carry out the functions of the state. Guns, big and small, were the order of the day and armed conflicts were a daily occurrence. There were we, unarmed, in the middle of two fighting groups, trying to bring about peace and do the work for which we had been trained. We walked and cycled the country roads of Ireland, we met with the plain people of Ireland on the roads and in the fields at their work, we discussed with them every possible topic of rural life, including farming and social activities such as football, hurling, handball and athletics generally.

We entered their houses, danced with and courted their daughters. We attended their country dances held in their own homes – dancing then was not legalised or commercialised. We danced sometimes until the small hours of the morning. We took off our tunics and danced at the crossroads, dancing throughout the country roads of Ireland. Policemen were never too favourably received in Ireland. How did we break down those barriers of suspicion and hatred of police, fostered, nurtured and developed on the plain people of Ireland by poor Mother England, whose policy insofar as Ireland was concerned was to divide and conquer?

The ordinary men and women of Ireland were in the vanguard of every movement for the freedom of our country down the ages and we were resolved that once we became involved in their affairs we were assured of success. We joined their football, hurling and handball clubs and were gladly accepted, not because we were young men of the civic guard or were of fine physique but because we could blooming well play hurling, football and handball as well, if not better, than the most of them. We played in their competitions and walked and cycled to the sports venues – this was before the advent of the motor car. We thus became involved in every possible way in Irish life and were heartily received and became very popular with the people with whom we came into contact.

In that way we won our way into the homes and the hearts of the Irish people and thus succeeded in accomplishing the ordinary police work we set out to do. I should mention that we broke down those barriers of suspicion and distrust despite the fact that we inherited the most tyrannical disciplinary code of regulations from the RIC – the worst that could be imposed on any police force in the world, which contained such clauses as 'Undue Familiarity', 'Gossiping while on Duty' and 'Gambling'.

The large number of clergy present at this function has a special significance: down the years from the very foundation of the gardaí, very close bonds of ties and friendship have been kept by Church and State here in Tipperary. The gardaí have made sizeable contributions to that happy union, which has been exemplified in the church ceremonies this evening. We were honoured and privileged to have a special place in front of the high altar to watch eight priests, all sons of our members, assist at Holy Mass under the fatherly guidance of His Grace, our beloved archbishop, a religious ceremony unique in the ecclesiastical history of the cathedral in the town of Thurles.

May God bless and preserve those young priests in the field of Catholicism and may their reward be as fruitful in the spiritual sphere as that of their fathers, here present, in the service of the Garda Síochána. They brought credit and honour to their parents present, and indeed it was a very proud occasion for all of us. Brevity has been the dominant factor of the other speakers before me – my apologies for transgressing this essential rule on the occasion of a social gathering. I had to give you some hard additional facts of our experience at the beginning of the Garda Síochána.

In case I say too much, let me finish. Fifty years ago, we were honoured and privileged to go out as young boys of the civic guard under our native government. We established tra-

> ditions of dedication to service and loyalty to the several functions of the State and developed a spirit of comradeship that we have now handed on to the younger men of the Garda Síochána, manifested here tonight by the officers and men of Tipperary who organised this beautiful banquet in our honour.

When eventually he sat down, the entire assembly was on its feet in acclamation. Many people, including the VIPs, left their tables to shake his hand and afterwards, as he moved through the crowds, it was the same. Quips such as, 'You should head straight for the Park!' 'Any chance you'd go into politics?' and 'There was a great missioner lost in you' were heard. It was a *tour de force* and a night to remember.

There was one sergeant in particular who charmed his way into the hearts of the community. He had, in his own words, 'a strong wakeness for the dhrop'. This yearning was at its most fervid when the wind was blowing from the east. As there was no pub in the village, he would make his way up to the post office on the pretext of mailing a few official letters. My mother, the postmistress, often recounted one such visit.

'Sergeant, will you have a little drop of the crathur?' she asked him.

'Tell me first, Mrs Feehan, what way is the wind blowing?' he replied.

'Well now, sergeant, I think it is coming from the east.'

'Then in that case, Mrs Feehan, I shall acquiesce to your kind and generous offer. Though mind you,' he added, 'that pernicious liquid has, as you well know, broken more hearts, blighted more hopes and rent asunder family ties more than anything since the Great Famine of Black '47.'

Pausing to see what effect this flight of oratory had on my mother, he continued, 'Still and all, I'll have a gargle, though I feel I must tell you, Mrs Feehan, that my normal attitude towards the said liquor is one of a studied animosity!' With which astute remark he downed his antidote to the east wind.

Shortly afterwards the sergeant was transferred to Dublin, and deep, sepulchral gloom descended on our little village. In those days Clery's ran cheap shopping excursions to Dublin from nearby Laffan's Bridge. One could travel return by train for a mere three shillings. On each of these scheduled expeditions a number travelled for the express purpose of meeting the sergeant. When the cortège arrived in O'Connell Street, one of them on his maiden visit to the capital city approached a garda who was busy directing traffic.

'How's the sergeant?' he asked, to which the garda, visibly annoyed at this intrusion, retorted, 'What sergeant?'

'The one we sent ye up.'

'And where, might I ask, did ye send him from?'

'From Ballinure, where else?' replied the rural pilgrim, surprised at this apparent display of ignorance.

'And where in God's name is Ballinure?'

This was the last straw. The traveller shook his head sadly and sighed, 'Where's Ballinure? Christ, you sir, you must have been born in Aygipt!'

The garda station in Ballinure was closed in 1970 in the interests of so-called rationalisation and it has remained empty since. It is interesting to note that the Garda Training Centre in Templemore, reputed to be one of the best of its kind in the world, is named after and dedicated to Pierce McCan, the man arrested by the RIC.

4

Knights of the Road

Growing up in a country post office brought us into contact with the knights of the road – loveable characters who once roved the Munster countryside but have now disappeared like the snows of yesteryear. An honest tribe they were, who slept in hay barns and were hospitably received by the farm housewife. They called to the post office to receive the few shillings that might, or might not, be coming to them from a parsimonious state. On Fridays – pension day – they would call in hopeful expectation of sharing in the largesse of the pensioners, who would be sure to give them a few coppers from their ten-shillings weekly allowance. Chalk pipes cost just a penny and they would negotiate with my mother for 'a half quarter of tobaccy', which they generally received at a generous discount.

A frequent visitor was 'Mickey Tuesday', a stooped old man from God-knows-where, whose headquarters were in Twin Burke's lodging house in a Cashel lane. Mickey had a fixed weekly programme. On Mondays he regularly visited Rosegreen, where he was known as 'Johnny Monday'. On Wednesdays he walked the roads of Boherlahan and Tubberadora and was known to the people of that district as 'Tommy Wednesday'. Friday was his day for visiting the country post offices, where he became known as 'Willie Friday'. Mickey rested on Sundays.

Denis O'Sullivan and John O'Connell, two of our senior parishioners, recall seeing Mickey walking along the road beating himself with a stout blackthorn stick and so, as he thought, driving the evil spirit out of his body.

Sammy the Horse Trainer was a familiar sight on the roads of South Tipperary. He was usually attired in a tall hat and cut-away coat and decorated in season with a large red rose. The story goes that in his early days he was a horse trainer whom bad luck and misfortune had driven onto the roads. He had an acerbic wit and a scathing tongue for cutting people with pretentious airs down to size. One of his victims was a bumptious character with lofty political aspirations who got himself elected as a member of a local district council. This man was so chuffed by the honour that he foolishly sought Sammy's approval of the people's choice.

'Did you hear that I was elected a member of the Cashel Rural District Council?' he asked.

'I did, sir,' was the reply.

'And what did you think of it, Sammy?'

'Well, sir,' replied Sammy, 'I suppose every circus is entitled to its clown!'

The knights who roamed the roads of Tipperary in the olden days were legion. We remember 'Lahy the Lawyer', 'Con So-Ho', Denis Kilmerney, Paddy Franklin, 'Seamus Forty Coats' and John O'Dargan, 'The Scobber', with a bell on his blackthorn stick and the capacity to twist his face into a seemingly infinite variety of contortions. But all of these freely admitted that the king and supreme knight of the roads had to be 'Paddy the Barrow'.

Paddy was the best-known of all the wandering characters who trod the roads of Munster in the first two decades of the last century. When I came to my present parish in the mid-1980s I had the good fortune to meet a lady who had good reason to remember Paddy the Barrow. Mary Finn on her ninety-ninth birthday asked me to say Mass in her home in Dualla. Afterwards, as we reminisced about old times, she came out with the pearl of great price that I had been seeking.

'I remember Paddy the Barrow well!' she mused. 'He had a huge wheelbarrow which he pushed before him, and in it he carried his blankets and personal wardrobe, as well as the potatoes, Indian meal, and bread and meat which he collected in farmhouses. Now, mind you, he'd only go into farmhouses like ours that were in a bit off the roads and he'd lie down in the hay barn for the night.

'He'd sell the potatoes and meal to the cottagers and, when he had one hundred and twenty pence, he exchanged them in a shop for a half-sovereign in gold. He used to wear several trousers, vests and coats at the same time and, when my mother would ask why, he'd say that he wore them to make himself look fat.

'Well one evening, when I was about eight, we were having our tea when my mother, looking out the window, spotted Paddy the Barrow making for the hay barn. She brought him out a mug of tea and something to go along with it.

'Well anyway,' she continued, 'when I saw him goin' through the yard he had on him the funniest-lookin' hat you ever saw in your life. And I was determined that I was goin' to see it at close quarters. So the next morning I got up early and out I went to the hay barn and there he was fast asleep in the hay, wearin' the hat, I thank you. So I got a bit of a *cipín* (a small stick) and I started to manoeuvre it off his head, when he woke up and, seeing what I was up to, made after me. I ran screamin' through the yard, and as soon as my mother came to the kitchen door Paddy shouted to her. "Catch her, missus, catch her – she's fat enough to kill her!" But sure he was only coddin' the poor crathur and we were the best of friends afterwards.'

Then she told me that Paddy, in his old age, was found one cold winter's day frozen to death in a hay barn near Midleton, County Cork. He was brought to the county home, where no fewer than 130 half-sovereigns were found securely sewn into his ragged clothes.

Mickey Connors, like Melchizedech of old, had neither kith nor kin. No one knew where he came from, but he lived in and around Ballinure for as long as everyone could remember. He never had a home that he could call his own and had to depend on the charity of the people for the roof over his head – which more often than not was a farm outhouse or a hay barn. He stayed with us for a number of years, living in a loft at the back of the dwelling. During this time he was part of the family, sharing our joys and sorrows and kneeling with us to say the family rosary at night. Years afterwards, he used remind us of these happy days when he rocked our cradles and, as he said himself, 'reared' us.

I can recall a scene from my childhood when he took me aside and said to me, 'I want you to do me one favour. When you grow up and become a priest, say one Mass for me when I'm dead and gone.' Every time I came home on holidays from the seminary, he repeated the request, and he again reminded me before I left for New Zealand, 'I'll be gone when you come home again – but don't forget to say that Mass for me.' I was never to see Mickey again. He was found dead in an outhouse without even a bed to lie on; without a local priest to anoint him or even officiate at his graveside. The old slur: high money, high Mass; low money, low Mass; no money, no Mass was verified in this particular instance. But Mickey had no need of the ministrations of the clergy. The very texture of his daily life was shot through with the luminous fibre of constant communing with God. His fidelity to his Mass bordered on the heroic. Hail, rain or snow, his familiar figure could be seen on the road, walking the long, weary miles to the chapel, and long before the priest appeared on the altar, he was in his place communing with God; passing through his fingers a well-worn rosary beads or reading above his breath from a thumb-blackened prayer book. So too he trudged his way back to Ballinure to break his fast at midday with a frugal meal.

And Mickey was not without his funeral Mass, albeit 12,000 miles from Ballinure! I fulfilled his request in St Joseph's Church, Wellington, and told his story to my first parishioners. What I said on the occasion was printed in the parish newspaper. I found the clipping recently in an envelope amongst my mother's memorabilia. On the cover was the simple message, 'Re. poor Mickey Connors. Don't throw this away. Keep it. Poor Mickey was good to everyone.'

5

Treasure Hidden in a Field

It was planned and built long long ago in Ireland's Golden Age,
By the Gobán Saor himself, that wise and gifted sage.
And to ensure that for posterity his treasures might endure,
They were laid to rest in Lurgoe, not far from Ballinure.

The Kingdom of Heaven is like treasure hidden in a field. Thus spoke the Lord about his kingdom on this earth (Matthew 13:44), but Andrew Finn, our local poet laureate, had different treasures in mind when he penned the above lines in the 1930s. He was giving voice to the common belief at the time that there were treasures hidden in Derrynaflan, a raised island in Lurgoe Bog, known to us simply as the Gobán Saor's Island. Following the find of the Derrynaflan Hoard in 1980, about which more anon, Davy Cormack, the well-known songwriter and 'Bard of Ardagh', had this to say:

O'er Allen I flew, and beneath did I scan
The beautiful island of Derrynaflan.
'Twas there Gobán Saor hid the chalice from all
Near the part of Slieveardagh that's called Killenaule.

I should mention that Davy, with whom I served Mass, and who is now gone to God, was unashamedly partisan in all matters relating to Killenaule. Derrynaflan is much closer to Ballinure, but who am I to talk, since all three locations belong to the parish that proudly calls itself Killenaule!

My interest in Derrynaflan goes back six decades, to my school days in Rockwell College. Father Reggie Walker, editor of the *Rockwell Annual*, asked me to write a feature on the Gobán Saor. 'The Gobán Saor,' he said, 'is buried on that island in the bog. Find out all you can about him. Take a few pictures of the monastic ruins and report back to me.'

My quest began, not on the island, but straight across the road in the home of our nearest neighbours: Mun (short for Edmund) and Hannie Bulfin. Theirs was a *cuaird dtigh-each* house where the neighbours gathered at night to chat and tell stories. 'Come and sit at the fire' was Hannie's greeting to all comers. The open-hearth fire was the centre and heart of the Bulfin homestead. During the day it was functional: bread had to be baked and pots had to be boiled for dinner and the pigs and the hens and woe betide anyone who sat around the fire during its functional uses. My father learned this to his cost one afternoon when he called to Mun with a book. Avid readers both, they became so engrossed in discussing literature that they failed to notice Hannie's growing annoyance as she elbowed her way between them to check on the pot-oven bread that she baked every day. When Mun finally sensed her displeasure, he turned to my father with a wink, saying, 'Tom, what's this Shakespeare had to say about women?'

Hannie turned on him in exasperation, 'To the Divil with you and Shakespeare, 'tis Shakespeare have you as you are!' And then she went on in even more explosive terms to tell him exactly what he was!

In the evening it was a more relaxed fire, however. Here the neighbours gathered and to the chirping of crickets in the hob they told tales of other days – tales of wakes and weddings, banshees and ghosts. Of course everybody's grandmother had heard the banshee and seen a ghost.

Some of the stories lost nothing in the telling, like the party over in Ballinaglera where 'four men for four days were stripped to the waist, mixin' the mustard for the sandwiches!'

Then it was time to go, but first the fire had to be raked. A few hard sods of turf would ensure a blazing fire. The fire was the link between today and tomorrow: it was life and continuity. The old day died with its rakings and the new day began with its kindlings. The fire, with its power, was the ever-present constant in the midst of change from dusk to dawn and from dawn to dusk.

It was at one of these fireside gatherings that I first broached the subject of Derrynaflan to Hannie. She was now a widow just turned ninety and the oldest person in the village. By birth she was a Nolan from Lurgoe and it was on family land that the hoard – chalice, paten and strainer – were discovered. But the discovery was forty years into the future when I spoke to her. Bear in mind that she was born and raised in this now-famous location and the memories that she recreated for me that evening went back to the middle of the nineteenth century.

First she told me stories about the Gobán Saor, which was the primary purpose of my visit. Then she came up with two fascinating stories about the Mrs Gobán – one of them telling how the master craftsman met his future wife. The story goes as follows.

When the Gobán was a *garsún* his father gave him the skin of a sheep to sell, telling him to dispose of it to some young woman who'd be prepared to give him the skin and the price of it. His search proved fruitless until one day, when he met a girl who was prepared to give him a price for the skin and then return it to him. She then proceeded to shear the sheep for its wool and gave it back to him. When he returned with the skin and its price, the father said to him, 'Now, lad, that's the girl for you. Seek her out and ask her to be your wife'. So the Gobán set off and once again met the woman of his dreams, whom he wooed and wed and then escorted back to Derrynaflan.

A master builder, the Gobán is credited with the construction of many of the churches and monuments of Munster. In this he was assisted by eleven journeymen whom he had recruited and trained. With their assistance, he acquired fame and fortune – so much so that, driven by jealousy, they conspired against him and eventually robbed and killed him. The wife, however, upholding the proudest traditions of her sex, had the last word. She procured a large tree sawn down the middle and kept partly separated by a wedge at the open end. On the pretext of altering the wedge, she got the men, six on one side and five on the other, to keep the slit separated as it was. Then she removed the wedge and the eleven assassins found themselves grasped by the fingers, as if in a vice. She then calmly proceeded to sharpen an axe and then complacently chopped off the heads of her husband's murderers. Their bodies were buried in a large mound beside the church. Further down the slope towards the north are the graves of the Gobán, his wife and their two children. At least that is how the legend goes.

When Hannie had finished her stories about the Gobán, she looked at me and said, 'I'm telling you, Jimmy, there's more than graves there. Mark my words, there's treasure buried on that island!'

'Is there?' I gasped. 'Do you know where it is?'

She nodded her head and went on, 'You mightn't have to dig too deep to find it.'

When I repeated my query about the treasure's whereabouts, she just pursed her lips and said, 'It's better to let that die with the old people. We have respect for sacred things. We wouldn't lay a wet finger on them!'

Forty years later, an Englishman and his son, with the aid of a metal detector, did lay their hands on them. The rest is history.

Jack Nolan, Hannie's nephew, was the owner of the island when I visited it to gather material for the *Rockwell College Annual*. Jack, now ninety-two, is a mine of information on the historic site. He is also a life-long friend of mine: he was a daily visitor to my home on his way to the local creamery. He sold the land shortly before the discovery of the hoard and moved to Holycross with his wife, Sadie, who died in the recent past. He told me that he brought Sadie to Derrynaflan shortly after they first met and how they sat together on a low stone wall with their feet resting on the famous hoard just six inches below the surface. 'And it took two Englishmen to find it,' he reminisced. Jack too believed his aunt's story about the hidden treasure.

Derrynaflan has a long history. It may have been anciently connected with the druids before St Ruadhan of Lorrha founded a monastery there in the sixth century. It later became the abode of the Céile Dé movement – monks intent on reforming and recapturing the spirit of the original monastic settlements by acting as a leaven through the austerity and simplicity of their lives. At some stage in the Middle Ages Derrynaflan ceased to be a monastery and it is listed in the fourteenth century as a parish church in the deanery of Slieveardagh. It became a ruin shortly afterwards and, apart from a brief spell in the middle of the seventeenth century when it was occupied by Franciscan monks fleeing from the Cromwellian massacre in Cashel, the place has been virtually a ruin ever since. There are the remains of two churches, one very ancient, certainly seeming to be of the twelfth century. The other, with lancet windows, suggests a more modern style.

Jesus, when comparing the Kingdom of Heaven to treasure hidden in a field, would have had no problem identifying with the hidden treasures of Derrynaflan – hidden lest they fell into the hands of marauding Danes or Norsemen. In the culture in which he lived and preached, people knew for centuries what it was to pack up in the middle of the night and leave their farms and homesteads because of the threatened invasion of some army on the march. Quite often a man would hastily bury his life's savings in the ground, hoping one day to come back and recover his wealth. More often than not, he never returned, leaving it for someone else in the future to stumble upon unexpected hidden treasure.

Storytellers were very popular in Palestine and, like Hannie Bulfin and Jack Nolan, there was nothing people liked better than a story of buried treasure. So they must have been all ears when Jesus told them stories of the treasure hidden in the field and the pearl of great price. These are the shortest stories Jesus ever told, each of them getting just one verse of Scripture:

> The Kingdom of Heaven is like treasure hidden in a field, which a man found and covered up; then in his joy he goes

> and sells all that he has and buys the field; again the Kingdom of Heaven is like a merchant in search of fine pearls, who, on finding one pearl of great value, went and sold all that he had and bought it (Matthew 13:44–5).

If we form a composite of these two stories we find five key words: he searched, he found, he rejoiced, he sold and he bought. The people latched on to Christ's story of the farmer whose plough struck something hard in the ground, which proved to be an old chest full of coins and precious stones. 'Go on,' they said, 'tell us what happened next.'

Now notice the masterly way Jesus relates this story to the life experience of those listening to him. Using compelling imagination, he draws his hearers into his own faith experience. The sequence of searching, finding, rejoicing, buying and selling was an authentic life experience for all of them, so Jesus goes on: because the price of the field was high, the man had to sell everything he had to raise enough cash, but it was worth it. He just had to have that treasure!

The people got the point, and no doubt some of them gave up their false gods of consumerism, materialism and selfishness so that they might have instead the treasures of the Kingdom of God. And remember the prophetic advice of Hannie Bulfin sixty years ago: you mightn't have to dig deep to find the treasure. So true, if the treasure we are seeking is a new relationship with God, then, for many of us, like the hoard of Derrynaflan, it will be found beneath the surface of our daily lives, but only in Christ and through Christ, in whom are hid all the treasures of wisdom and knowledge (Colossians 2:3).

6

Odyssey of a Spoiled Priest

The odyssey began in September 1942, when I set out on the long trek to the priesthood that would end – or so I thought – with ordination and the purging of ghosts in 1950. What should have been a real odyssey, an adventurous journey towards the realisation of a dream, was clouded from the start by my father's refusal to bid me farewell on the day I set out for the seminary. As the time for my departure drew near, the silence between us grew more and more oppressive, until finally he left the house in a huff, muttering to my mother as he went, 'He's just going to be another spoiled priest like the rest of them.'

'What's a spoiled priest?' I asked her, when she related the incident to me.

'Oh, it's what they call someone who doesn't persevere or who has been put out of the seminary, and the stigma and disgrace that goes with it. But don't mind him, *alanna,* he'll come around.'

'But who are the rest of them?' I continued.

'Well, there were two nephews of his up in Offaly – one in the Jesuits and the other in the Holy Ghost Order. They came out. And then of course there was Seán,' she mused, referring to my brother's brief sojourn in the Holy Ghost Novitiate. 'He's afraid you're going to do the same,' she went on, 'and I'll tell you something else, *alanna,* but promise me you won't breathe a word of it.'

I nodded to reassure her.

'He spent a while himself as a Franciscan Brother up in Clara but nobody knows this and he'd kill me if he thought I'd told you. Now, he firmly believes that there's a curse on the family where vocations are concerned.'

I paused for a moment to digest all of this and tot up the tally of failures. 'So I'm going to be the Fifth Sorrowful Mystery?' I ventured.

'You're not, *alanna,*' she reassured me. 'I prayed every day for you since you were a child that you'd be a priest and say the Mass in black over me when I die.'

I waited until the last minute to see would he return, but he didn't. There was no one to drive me, as cars were off the road and our Baby Ford had been languishing in the garage since shortly after the outbreak of the Second World War in 1939. One of the neighbours took me to the station in Laffans' Bridge in a pony and trap. I really felt like an anachronism when I got off the train in Thurles, outfitted in black overcoat, black suit and black hat, and trudged through the town, lugging a large suitcase and praying that nobody would recognise me. At last I reached the entrance. When passing between the two golden eagles on the college gateposts my heart sank when I saw the grey forbidding edifice looming before me at the end of the avenue.

Gathered on the steps in front of the hall door, awaiting more newcomers, was a group of my future colleagues, amongst them names that would be forever etched in my heart and memories: James Meehan, who would earn the appellation 'the Champion of the Poor'; Louis Gleeson, who would accompany me on the great adventure to New Zealand; Dick Doheny, happily still with us in Sacramento, California; and dear, jovial Dick Meagher from Templemore, who, seeing me in a state of sheer exhaustion after the long tramp from the station, took my suitcase, saying, 'Follow me' and then whispered into my ear, 'This place lacks the feminine touch!' How right he was. The hallway and main corridor were draped with old musty oil paintings, with their motley selection of church dignitaries glowering down on the new crop of students.

The president, Father Richard Devane, came down to greet us, addressing each one formally as 'Mister'. He told us that those aspiring to ministry on the home mission would be assigned to the rhetoric class to pursue a course of studies in preparation for the Concursus in June. The Concursus, a written examination by another name, would determine which of use would be selected for service in the archdiocese. We would not be allocated rooms like the philosophy and theology students. Instead we were assigned to dormitories. The other freshmen who opted for service on the foreign missions joined the first philosophy class, where they were introduced to a new range of subjects that were totally alien to many of them, as evidenced in an amusing incident that first evening in the outside toilets, when two of them, one being Dick Meagher, were side by side, ridding themselves of superfluous liquids. The other, in his naivety, asked Dick, 'What's "epistemology"?'

'It's what you're doing now' was the riposte of the philosopher from Templemore.

Lights were put out at 9.30 pm, followed by strict, solemn silence until after breakfast. The main body of students arrived the following day. Then we were thrust into a three-day retreat, after which we were to discover what it meant to be a rhetoric student. It was just a rehash of the secular studies we had pursued the previous year. In retrospect, it was an irrelevant and wasted year, now thankfully long since discarded. It did, however, introduce us to meditation, spiritual reading and spiritual direction, but our peers from all other Irish dioceses were already in Maynooth pursuing courses in arts and philosophy. We would follow a year later, our studies stunted rather than advanced by the year in rhetoric. After the Concursus in June, four were selected for free places in Maynooth: Louis Gleeson, James Meehan, Tim O'Brien and myself.

When the four of us arrived in Maynooth in September 1943 we were joined by Tom Carroll from Thurles, who had won a university scholarship in the Leaving Certificate examination of the previous June. We were one of the biggest classes ever to enter the National Seminary: eighty-six in all. The junior dean welcomed us with an ominous note, telling us that it would be too much to expect that all of us would persevere to the end and that the gates were always open if we wanted to leave.

Coming from Thurles, we knew what to expect: up at 6 am, regular room inspections, no radios, newspapers or excursions to the secular city. The prevailing policy was seclusion from the contaminants of the secular world. We were going to live and minister in a world of sin and evil. We would not always be protected from temptations, moral and intellectual, but we should not be exposed to such temptations until we had been inoculated against them. The inoculation process began with isolation from the outside world.

Let me tell you of my one and only visit to the secular

city. At the halfway stage in my passage to the priesthood, I broke my glasses. This necessitated a trip to Dublin to have them repaired. This was not quite as simple as it sounds. The complex procedure began with a visit to Dr Gerry Montague, the dean. I explained the situation to him, pointing out that I could not read or study without my spectacles and would have to have them repaired immediately. He suggested that I was being 'singular' in looking for special privileges and that, furthermore, only the president was empowered to permit me to go to Dublin and only he, Dr Montague, was empowered to permit me to go to the president. After further questioning, he grudgingly gave me his assent to the next move.

I made my way to the presidential suite, where I was subjected to another grilling. 'I can't give you permission to go to Dublin,' the president told me, 'only your bishop can do that. Write to the bishop and them come back to me and we'll see.'

'But in the meantime, monsignor,' I said, 'I won't be able to see, or study or even write to my bishop without my glasses!'

'Oh all right then, you may go to see your optician, but bring me back a letter from your bishop ratifying this permit.'

I thanked him and returned to the dean with the good news. He was not impressed and needed to be reassured that I was not looking for special privileges.

Next day I had to sign in at the college lodge, entering the time of my departure. Then I caught the 10 am bus to the city, had my glasses repaired and returned to Maynooth, signing in again at the lodge. I was then obliged to go to the dean and notify him that I was now officially back in the college.

The final stage of this ridiculous saga was writing to my bishop, explaining the circumstances of my trip to the city and seeking his ratification. This arrived in due course and I brought it to the president, having first gone to the dean to seek permission to visit the presidential quarters. And all of this just to have my glasses repaired!

Books by 'unapproved authors' were strictly forbidden. This was quite an obsession of Dean Gerry Montague. When the dean came to our rooms on regular visitations, you could sense his eyes scanning the bookshelves, looking for evidence of unapproved authors. Seán Corkery, a priest of Ardagh diocese, spent some years in Africa with the missionaries of St Patrick's Missionary Society, Kiltegan. On his return to Ireland, he was appointed librarian in Maynooth College. On one memorable occasion, when it was his turn to be chief celebrant at Sunday Mass in the college chapel, he bellowed out an *Ite Missa Est* that flummoxed both organist and choir and left them convulsed with laughter. Later, when he entered the professor's dining-room for lunch, Gerry Montague was waiting for him.

'Well, Seán,' Gerry chortled, 'it may not have been *Bel Canto,* but it was certainly *Can Belto.'*

This provoked another peal of laughter from the confrères but, not to be out-witted, Corks, as he was known to all and sundry, came out with a brilliant riposte. 'Now, Gerry, let me tell you of another occasion when I found myself in a very sensitive and embarrassing situation. I was saying an open-air Mass one Sunday in Kenya when a bloody bee went up the leg of my pants. I could feel the hoor creeping stealthily towards a rather sensitive area when I rushed from the altar and made for a small tent that served as a sacristy.'

'And what did you do when you got there, Seán?' said Gerry, a note of concern in his voice.

'Sure Gerry, what could I do in the circumstances. I looked up the approved authors!'

Particular friendships were discouraged. You consorted only with your fellow diocesans or students of your own class and you were forbidden entry into another student's room. This struck at the very heart of fraternity – a core value of our priesthood. The downgrading of fraternity was also reflected in the monolithic system of apartheid that existed between priests and students. The priests on the staff passed you on the corridors with stony visages and never a word of greeting, and if you ventured to greet any one of them you could expect a chilly glance from the passing don. 'Surely to God,' a classmate recalled, 'we were entitled at the very least to a shared humanity, a realisation that if God became Man, then men – and especially priests – should act like human beings.'

Our seminary period was a time for stifling our feelings, seeing how long they could be kept invisible. Girls and ladies of every vintage were referred to as members of the opposite sex and were forbidden territory, but if you suppress and conceal your deepest feelings you store up trouble for later.

The trouble began for me sooner rather than later, and it started with a kiss. It was in the early days of my seminary life. Now bear in mind when appraising what follows that my sheltered life, both at home and in Maynooth, was such that I'd never been to a dance, never had a date and never been kissed. During one of my early Christmas holidays I had gone to see the film *How Green Was My Valley,* based on Richard Llewelyn's classic novel of the same name. It was the story of the childhood and youth of Huw Morgan, a miner's son in a south Wales valley.

The chapel dominated the valley, a Methodist house of worship built by the miners where Huw spent five hours every Sunday between morning service, afternoon Sunday school and evening service. Huw was very close to the new preacher, Mr Guffydd, and it came as no surprise that he had his sights set on the ministry. Then he met Bronwen, and the first kiss came in the romantic setting of the song of the nightingale and a full moon shedding its rays on the green mountain. It affected me deeply, so much so that I bought the book, never bothering to enquire if Richard Llewelyn was an approved author. Anyway, this is what Huw had to say about that famous first kiss:

> 'Good night, Bron,' I said, and kissed her quietly upon the mouth, and ran. There is strange, and yet not strange, is the kiss. It is strange because there is good reason of it. There is wonder for me that we kiss, for when mouth comes to mouth, in all its silliness, breath joins breath, and taste joins taste, warmth is enwarmed, and tongues commune in a soundless language, and those things are said that cannot find a shape, have a name or know a life in the pitiful faults of speech.

My first kiss was somewhat similar to Huw's – not quite as exploratory as his commentary might suggest, but beautiful nevertheless. My Bronwen (name concealed to protect the innocent!) was a raven-haired beauty in her middle teens.

Whereas Huw ran after his close encounter, I walked ... up to my knees in stardust! I was soon brought down to earth, however, when I returned to Maynooth and confessed the matter to my spiritual director.

'How often did it happen?' he asked.

'Just once, Father,' I replied.

He hummed and hawed for a short while before delivering judgement. 'Well, son, if it happens again, you should seriously consider whether you should continue on for the priesthood.'

I was simply shattered, and the thought that kept recurring during the sleepless nights that followed was: My God, I am just one kiss away from becoming a spoiled priest!

Bronwen – my one, that is – is happily married with children and grandchildren of her own. Fifty years after that single solitary kiss, her family decided to commemorate the event with a Christmas party, and there, under branches of mistletoe, we were asked to give a repeat performance. Which we did – only this time I did not tell it in Confession.

Another incident where sexuality raised its ugly head and blighted a promising musical career concerns two of my classmates, James Meehan and the future Bishop of Limerick, Jer Newman. James returned to the college after the summer vacation with a violin, and every day after dinner he would retire to his room and assiduously practice the scales and the few airs with which he was familiar, much to the chagrin of Jer Newman, who, in the room across the corridor, was with equal diligence preparing a thesis for an MA in philosophy. The scraping sounds of the fiddle to the future bishop were like the screaming of the damned in hell. Time and time again he would rush across to James' room totally distraught and plead with him to 'For God's sake stop scratching that blasted fiddle!' The budding maestro would then assume a look of wounded innocence but then, in the belief that the claims of music were greater than those of philosophy, would continue with the tortuous sounds as soon as Jer was back at this desk. Then one day the violin practices suddenly ceased, never to be resumed. As James practised on the offending instrument, the bishop-to-be strode into his room, brandishing a tome from which he read a passage by Sigmund Freud asserting that the primary function of the fiddle was to provide an outlet for sexual repression. James roundly placed the blame for this *coup de grâce* on his promising musical career not on his colleague in the room opposite but on 'that auld Freud lad out in Vienna'.

Creativity was also discouraged. One of our classmates was expelled for writing the story of Thomas Aquinas in novel form. After he left, the book, *Time Cannot Dim,* became a best-seller. Another, who was disciplined for the 'grave irregularity' of writing poetry, spoke in retrospect of those Ice Age years: 'Poetry was a forbidden craft in Maynooth, which was a prohibition which I could not understand, because poets never gave any trouble to the Church, which is more than can be said for many of the Popes.'

A notable exception to all this codology was James G. McGarry, our professor of homiletics. As if he foresaw the immanence of the communications revolution, he told us more than once that we were passing from a word culture to a picture culture and that the challenge facing us would be to get the message across to the pews in creative and imaginative language. 'That's how the Lord himself got the message across,' he once said in one of his lectures. 'The parables as Jesus told them were from real life: stories about farmers and fishermen, weddings and wakes, self-righteous humbugs and prodigal sons, stories that related to the real-life experiences of the Jews in the first century. That will be the challenge facing all of us in our homilies – to break through the shackles of time and make the same stories relevant in our own times. This calls for creativity and imagination.'

To be regarded as a sound man was the ultimate accolade in the Maynooth of our times – the ideal to which all of us aspired. It meant that we were well regarded by our peers and superiors but, as many of us were later to discover, the hallmark of the sound man in the 1940s and 1950s was mediocrity.

In a recent gathering of our class of 1950, part of our golden-jubilee celebrations, there was a general consensus that we had left Maynooth with a poor knowledge of the Scriptures, due, in the main, to the exclusive emphasis on exegesis and textual criticism.

When the word 'exegesis' was first mentioned to us, a number of students were seen to bow their heads, thinking that it was another form of the Holy Name! Our professors, John O'Flynn (New Testament) and Michael J. Leahy (Old Testament), were meticulous about the words as we studied them in Greek and Hebrew – words that just never came to life. John O'Flynn discussed with us in great depth the mysterious Document Q. In explaining the similarities and omissions in the first three Gospels, scripture scholars are agreed that there was another written source containing the sayings of Jesus. This they called 'Q' after the German word 'quelle' (meaning 'source'). They claim that Document Q was written in Aramaic around the year 50, possibly by Matthew, and was used by Luke and Matthew in writing their Gospels. The document, if it ever did exist, has disappeared.

This is the background to the following lampoon which appeared in the *Echo,* the college underground magazine, just before our time:

A bunch of the boys were baggsing about
In the Biblical Institute
Some were playing the Pentateuch
And others were playing the flute,
When up jumps John O'Flynn and says:
'I'll bet my second best sou'
That none of you louts know the whereabouts
Of the Document known as Q'.

Then up jumps Mickey Joe Leahy
And in cultured tones said 'Whisht!
Namely ... therefore ... that is ... we hold
That the document doesn't exist;
And if it did it wouldn't agree
With Exodus 22
For the Sacred Text has nothing to say
About the Document known as Q!'

I often think of my friend Travers, in this context, and his heart-warming love of the Scriptures. I can still see him, Bible in hand, at an adult-education lecture which included the student body in St Patrick's College, Thurles. He was replying to a paper on the Scriptures given by a scripture scholar. 'This book to me,' he declared, 'is a life-giving book. Your words, Lord, are spirit and they are life. Every time I open this book I open it to find Christ!'

When I compare Travers to some of our erstwhile scripture professors the words of Mary Magdalene on Easter morning come graphically to mind: 'They have taken away my Lord, and I know not where they have laid him' (John 20:13).

Another topic on which there was general agreement was the dominance of a dead language, Latin, in our theological studies. All our textbooks for dogmatic theology, moral theology and canon law were in Latin. Our examinations, both oral and written, were in Latin. We even had to pray in Latin. I found this most difficult and frustrating when I started theology, as I hadn't seen a Latin textbook in four years – not since I had left secondary school – and now I was expected to be proficient in the language: to be able to read, write and converse in Latin. Thank God the Church finally woke up to this anomaly. Now a student can go through all his seminary days – even through his entire priesthood – without knowing one word of Latin. Of course it has its uses. I am one of those with mixed feelings about the total abandonment of Latin in the Mass. The Latin Mass was a great mainstay when travelling in countries where one was unfamiliar with the language, besides being an effective reminder of the universality of the Church.

Dies irae, dies illa: This caption is yet another example of the usefulness of Latin. It is a graphic description of the Day of Judgement, which it portrays as a day of wrath. There was one such day, which occurred annually in our time as students – a day of general judgement. It was the day of the 'Order List', the dread day when those who were deemed worthy were called to Orders and those deemed unworthy were rejected.

It was a terrible ordeal for all of us, because it was a bitter disgrace to be set aside or, in college slang, to be 'clipped'. The day of the Order List was always on a Friday, which came to be known as Black Friday. Even the young students in Junior House were not immune from judgement. They had their own day of reckoning, euphemistically called the Good Conduct List, but in effect another *dies irae*.

When Black Friday came around and the bell tolled, we all – well nigh 400 of us – trooped into the college chapel and sat in fear and trembling. On the stroke of the hour the three deans, the vice-president and the president came in solemn procession and took their places in the sanctuary facing the student body. Then the president began to call out rapidly in Latin the names of those selected *ad primam tonsuram* ('to first tonsure'). He passed on to porters, lectors, acolytes, exorcists; then came the higher orders: subdeacon, deacon and finally *ad presbyteratum* – 'to the priesthood'.

Names were called in order of seniority. Each of us had a seniority-class number – mine was 27 – so we knew when our names were due to be called. To be passed over was a major catastrophe which involved visiting your dean to be told why you were deemed unfit. This, in some instances, could result in expulsion. Not to be called to the priesthood was the ultimate disgrace: it meant that you were sent out into the world with a brand of shame as a 'spoiled priest'. Even though I was a deacon and reading my breviary, the last Order List held the same anticipatory fears for me, and it was only when I heard the words 'Jacobus Feehan, Cassilensis' that a palpable feeling of relief enveloped me.

Thank God the Order List is now replaced by a more humane ritual and those awful words 'spoiled priest' have long since disappeared from our vocabularies, but for me as Ordination Sunday approached there was one more ghost yet to be laid. The following letter sent by my father, which arrived on the eve of ordination and is before me as I write, says it all:

Ballinure
16 June 1950

My dear Jimmy
The great day is at hand when God calls you to perform that miracle of miracles – the Holy Sacrifice of the Mass. I need not assure you our happiness is supreme. We really don't know what we are doing. Your mother is crying for joy and, as for myself, like David of old I'm inclined to give a 'few steps' around my room, with the door closed, of course. Well, may God send his choicest blessings on you and give you the courage to face the awesome ceremony on Sunday and may he give you a superabundance of his grace to enable you to be a good holy priest.

Best love from Dad and Thomas

PS Your mother writes now.

Needless to say, this was the icing on the cake and I have treasured it all down the years.

On the evening before ordination I visited the grave of Professor Walter McDonald in the college cemetery and spent some time in prayer and reflection. I'll have more to say later about this extraordinary man. I was ordained a priest on the following day, 18 June 1950. The ordaining prelate was John Charles McQuaid, Archbishop of Dublin. There were eighty-four of us in all; this was certainly the biggest class in the latter half of the last century. Because of space restrictions, only four family members were permitted to attend the ceremony, but we managed to squeeze in a few extra. The first Mass on the following day had to be celebrated in Maynooth, and for all of us it was a dream of joy. After Mass, I returned to Ballinure to a wonderful welcome. The entire village turned out for my first public Mass in St Mary's church, Killenaule. Afterwards I had an aching arm from giving my blessing to each member of the vast congregation. I had a similar experience in Dualla the following Sunday. Most of the people in Ballinure attended Mass in Dualla. Killenaule was four and a half miles away, Dualla half that distance, so this experience was a veritable homecoming.

As my departure for New Zealand was more than three months distant, there was time to visit the homes of the people and savour the privilege of belonging to a believing community. We were living on the fringes of three parishes and seldom saw our own clergy, who were almost five miles away. They rarely came to see us and house visits were few and far between. And yet, despite this lack of contact with our priests, vocations prospered in the 1940s and 1950s, mainly, as I discovered in my current visitation, because every house was, in effect, a miniature church. Not that we were praying to him all the time – we weren't – but God must have had red ears, we spoke about him so often. Our every conversation was charged with his presence. Expressions like 'God bless the work' and 'God save all here' came readily to our lips. Vocations were like home-made bread: home-made because love-made.

Michael Condon, life-long friend and neighbour, was

the first in the village to respond to the call of the Lord. His ordination was an epochal event for those of us who were aspiring to the priesthood and religious life. He was a role model to follow, and follow in his footsteps a few of us did: three priests, two religious brothers and eight sisters from the village and its environs was a reasonable output from homes such as I've described.

At our ordination in June there were four ordained for service in the Archdiocese of Cashel, but such was the abundance of priests and the length of waiting lists that we had to seek missions abroad until there were vacancies for us at home. A few weeks before ordination, a young archbishop from New Zealand addressed the ordination class in Maynooth in a plea for volunteers to come and work in his diocese, the capital city of Wellington, where the Church was celebrating the first hundred years of its existence. It was still mission territory – a territory much larger than Ireland. Peter McKeefry, who later became the first ever Cardinal in New Zealand, was a dynamic personality. He so inflamed our hearts and fired out imaginations that it was small wonder that two of us, Louis Gleeson and I, responded to his call to witness to Christ even unto the uttermost parts of the earth.

7

Reflections on the High Seas

Friday 6 October 1950 was the day the great adventure began: the day our horizons stretched halfway around the globe, from the relatively closed communities of Clogher for Louis and from Ballinure for me. Louis and his brother Michael arrived at my home around midday and, after lunch and final farewells, we set out for Cobh. It was Threshing Day at Din Dwyer's and a large crowd had gathered at the cross for what must have been one of the last of the *meitheals* before the advent of the combine harvester. They waved at us as we passed. There was one final call to Denis O'Sullivan of the Buildings. This visit was of special import for both Louis and me: it was a family relationship for Louis and for me a haven of neighbourliness and the epitome of the homes of Tipperary, with the granny at the fireside thumbing her beads and showering us with blessings later as we left for Cobh. Michael piloted us, collecting a puncture on the way.

Having completed the departures formalities at the offices of the United States Lines, we spent our last night with my brother Seán and Mary, his wife, in nearby Rushbrooke. Next morning, to the chimes of the bells of Cobh cathedral ringing out 'Come Back to Erin', we left by tender to board the *SS America,* which was waiting for us in the deep water of the bay. Having been assigned our cabin, we went up on deck and nostalgically watched the ever-receding coastline of Ireland. We ran into rough seas and soon had our first taste of seasickness. Sumptuous meals were served on board but we were too ill to partake of them. Whilst Louis lay in misery on his bunk bed, I staggered up on deck again for the first of my reveries.

Leaning on the taffrail and intermittently feeding the fishes and seagulls with my regurgitations, I comforted myself by recalling the coffin ships that had traversed these same waters in the aftermath of the Great Famine. A commissioner of emigration in the United States wrote poignantly at the time, 'If crosses and tombs could be erected on the waters, the whole route of the emigrant vessels from Europe to America would long since have assumed the appearance of a crowded cemetery.' Travelling in the luxury of the flagship of the American merchant navy, our problems paled into insignificance when one reflected on those countless thousands whose departure from Cobh was to end in a rendezvous with death and burial in the depths of the sea.

Next day, Sunday 8 October, brought its own share of problems – ones for which our liturgical training in the seminary had not prepared us. A priest passenger was too ill to celebrate Mass, so Louis and I had to say three Masses in the cabin class. Louis said the 7 am Mass and I assisted him by holding the chalice to prevent it capsizing. Louis provided the same service for me at the 7.30 and 9 o'clock celebrations. I felt very ill and had to lean against the altar all the time. Distributing Holy Communion was a frightening experience. I found myself lurching about, almost toppling people as the ship heaved to and fro. At the end of the Mass my fingers were covered with a red substance. At first I thought it was blood – perhaps even stigmata – but then I realised that it was my first close contact with ladies' lipstick! (Cross my heart!)

The Mass brought us into contact with many of our fellow travellers. Some were returning to America, having visited Rome for the Holy Year jubilee celebrations; others were Irish-Americans who had been visiting the homeland; and still others were maiden voyagers like ourselves en route to New York to see relatives and friends.

When accepting our applications to work in his diocese, Archbishop McKeefry offered us a choice of three routes to New Zealand. We could travel through Suez, Panama or the United States. Four of my aunts had emigrated in their youth to America and had never returned to their native land. Two of them had settled in New York, one in Washington DC and one in Chicago. As I had never met any of them, my choice of route was naturally to travel via America. Although Louis had no relatives in America, he agreed to go along with my choice.

I was really looking forward to meeting Aunt Sarah and Aunt Molly. These two never married. They devoted their entire life to sending money and clothes parcels first to their parents and then to their siblings at home. They wrote to me on a regular basis, sending me dollars to put me through school and college.

John Healy of the *Irish Times* also had three aunts who emigrated to America, with his own mother. In his classic sociological study *Nineteen Acres,* he follows the family to America and chronicles the successes and failures of those who did not return. His mother, like her three siblings, emigrated to New York with the same parting phrase: 'Keep your mouth and your legs closed. Keep your eyes opened and send home the ticket for the next one.'

I asked myself what it must have been like for Aunt Sarah, the first to go, with a tag in her lapel from a small homestead in Lisnamrock, five miles from Ballinure, never having seen a town but when she passed on her way to Queenstown, and how she must have felt coming through Ellis Island to the polyglot city of New York a few weeks later. How did she survive? How did she prosper? For prosper she did. The Vanderbilts on Long Island wanted an Irish help and Sarah, with only the education she received in Lisnamrock school, went in as a domestic. As a result, the clothes parcels she sent home were of a superior quality, albeit the cast-offs of the Vanderbilts.

Molly's was a similar story. She too found domestic employment with a family not quite of the same social standing as the Vanderbilts, but they were shrewd financiers, nevertheless, who encouraged her to save and to invest wisely. These two remarkable sisters were the *raison d'être* for my journey on the *SS America*. Their selfless generosity was matched only by their heroic self-sacrifice in giving up their prospects of marriage and having homes of their own. The other sisters, both named Margaret – one a sister of my father, the other of my mother – settled down and had families of their own in Chicago and Washington. They too had written to me assuring me of a warm welcome in their homes.

On Tuesday 10 October I said the 7.30 am Mass in tourist class. Then I went to the ship's barber and had a haircut, which cost ninety cents. John, the barber, was a Catholic. He treated me to two glasses of Coca-Cola, a packet of Chesterfield cigarettes (although I don't smoke) and a packet of pipe tobacco. He also lent me a copy of the *Cardinal*. We ran into a storm in the evening. Being the month of October, it was my turn to lead the Rosary in the lounge, and there were chairs slipping all over the place. We had a gala dinner in the evening, at which we wore party hats and shook rattlers. We entered into the spirit of the occasion and enjoyed ourselves. We had great sport bursting balloons.

On Wednesday 11 October, having celebrated the 7.30 am Mass in cabin class, I played table tennis with Louis. Then I took John's copy of the *Cardinal* with me to the lounge and decided to get it read before we arrived in New York on Friday. Sitting opposite me, and also reading, was an elderly, distinguished-looking gentleman, who turned out to be Oliver St John Gogarty (1878–1957), physician, raconteur, poet, author of *As I Was Going Down Sackville Street* (1937) and student friend of James Joyce. He was so close to me that I could reach out and touch him but there were no overtures to converse from either side. Had I known at the time that I would become a friend and confidant of Joyce's sister in New Zealand, things might have been very different.

The friendship between Gogarty and Joyce soured not long after they moved into that strangest of residences, the Martello Tower at Sandycove, which Gogarty rented from the Secretary of State for War and paid the £8 annual rent. Joyce claimed that he was put out of the tower and he also blamed Gogarty for introducing him to drink with, as he claimed, malice aforethought. Gogarty tried to ingratiate himself with Joyce, fearing that he would be caricatured when his former friend became famous. His forebodings were realised when he found himself back in the Sandycove Tower as Buck Mulligan in the opening chapter of *Ulysses*.

Thursday 12 October was our last day at sea. I spent most of the day on deck reflecting on a man who made this same journey fifty years before. He was embarking on a lecture tour of the United States and would be invited back again in 1908. Professor Walter McDonald, DD, Prefect of the Dunboyne Establishment in Maynooth from 1888 to 1920, was a towering figure in the faculty of theology in the national seminary as it faced into the last century of the second millennium. In the then witch-hunt for anything that smacked of modernism, he fell foul of some of his colleagues, notably Dr Coughlan, the senior professor of dogmatic theology. Coughlan was responsible for McDonald's book, *Motion: Its Origin and Conservation*, being banned by the bishop trustees of the college and by the Sacred Congregation of the Index. Time has since vindicated McDonald. Many of his ideas, like that on motion, are now accepted as commonplace. He was a champion of the rights of the individual against the system, and with unfailing courage he proclaimed, rightly or wrongly, what he believed to be the truth. The final paragraph of his memoirs, *The Reminiscences of a Maynooth Professor*, is a fitting curtain call for a man whose sole desire was 'to tell the truth' in the interests of both the college which he loved and served with so much devotion and of the Irish Church as a whole, which he adorned as one of its brightest jewels:

> Episcophobia! Yes, I have faced bishops and their masters, being worsted in the conflict, and, as I believe, injured grievously. Not maliciously, however – the men who struck hard-

est at me did it in good faith. I do not blame them, nor desire to see them punished, however I may feel aggrieved. May they live long and rule happily, but may they be punished also, by having their eyes opened to the evil they have done unwittingly, not to me only – for that counts little – but to the cause of truth. The shame of such revelation, when it comes, as come it will, is more than enough of punishment.

'A model bishop, if ever there was one'. Such was Walter McDonald's tribute to one of the greatest missionary bishops of the past millennium. As we have seen, McDonald had some harsh things to say about some of the Irish bishops, but here was an Irish prelate whom he regarded as a role model. He met Laurence Scanlan during his 1900 tour of the United States. Here is the entry in McDonald's *Memoirs:*

> My next stop was at Salt Lake City, where I stayed in the house of Bishop Scanlan – a model bishop, if ever there was one. He worked and looked like any Irish curate ... I stayed with the bishop two days and learned to pity him for the great work he was trying to do, with very little help indeed.

Lawrence Scanlan has long been a hero and role model of mine, not least because he came from Ballytarsna, where I went to school, where my father taught school and which lies in the heart of the parish where I am now serving. The young Lawrence, who was born in the village on 28 September 1843, would later recall harrowing stories told by his parents of how, in the first ten years of his life, the population of the parish dropped from more than 7,000 souls to less than 2,000 through famine, fever, evictions and enforced emigration. Despite the severity of the times, Paddy and Kitty Scanlan, farming about a hundred acres of fertile land, were able to provide their children with a basic education in the only fee-paying school in the parish – a thatched cottage in Ballytarsna.

Lawrence later transferred to the monastery in Thurles, where, under the direction of Brother Francis Larkin, he excelled in English, mathematics and the classics. As the seeds of a call to the priesthood took root, he set his sights on the New World, and in particular the city behind the Golden Gate, San Francisco. After a brief spell in St Patrick's College, Thurles, he went to All Hallows College, Dublin, for his theological studies. Archbishop Joseph Alemany of San Francisco adopted him, as he needed priests to serve the increasing number of Irish who were settling in California. Lawrence was ordained at All Hallows on 24 June 1868. His first Mass in Boherlahan church was a dream of joy, not alone for the young priest but also for the priest who baptised him – William Kirwan, still hale and hearty and now in his thirty-ninth year as parish priest.

After a few weeks at home, Scanlan set sail on the long sea voyage to San Francisco. It would be another year before the trip across the American continent could be made by rail. As he embarked on the old steamship at Cobh and watched the receding coastline, he probably had no idea that he would never again see the land of his birth. When he arrived at New York, another tortuous sea journey awaited him, this time aboard a small steamboat bound for Panama. As the canal had not yet been constructed, he crossed the isthmus separating the Atlantic from the Pacific by land and then sailed on the Pacific Mail Steamship Company's line from Old Panama for San Francisco, where he was met by Archbishop Joseph S. Alemany.

As the Ballytarsna priest sailed through the famous

Golden Gate, catching his first glimpse of the City by the Bay, he saw a city that had undergone – and was still undergoing – a metamorphosis. First founded as a mission town by Spanish Franciscans in 1772, it was secularised by Mexico in 1833, and thirteen years later it and the entire state of California were annexed by the United States in its war with Mexico. In early 1848 gold was discovered about a hundred miles inland, in the Nevada foothills, and San Francisco was swiftly overwhelmed by a flood of humanity, wild with lust for sudden wealth.

After a few brief temporary appointments in the city early in 1869, less than a year after his ordination Lawrence Scanlan faced the first great challenge of his ministry. He was sent to Pioche, a rip-roaring mining camp in the hills of southern Nevada. Having travelled 300 miles by train and coach, he completed the journey on horseback, to be greeted by a motley crew of the wildest and toughest characters in the Wild West. These men, of all creeds and none, welcomed the young priest, and with their cooperation he soon built a frame church, with two rooms tacked on for living quarters. He took his meals in a Chinese 'chop suey'.

The third Sunday after he opened his little church, a deputation of miners waited upon him and firmly but respectfully intimated to him that his sermons were not suited to his environment. He had been preaching on the Four Last Things: Death, Judgement, Heaven and Hell. They told him to keep on telling them about heaven, but to leave out the other three, as these were unsuited to the time and place. Father Scanlan answered that he was not preaching his own opinions but the doctrines of Jesus Christ, the Son of God, and, he continued, 'While I am here, I'll preach Jesus Christ, and Him crucified.'

The miners boycotted him. The Chinese eating tent demanded cash for every meal. He was driven to beg a meal here and there, and his clothes began to lose colour and to resemble the garb of a tramp.

One afternoon, walking in the shade of the church, Dan O'Leary approached him. 'Father,' said Dan, shaking the priest by the hand, 'you've won out. The boys admire your pluck. Here's fifty dollars. Go down to Kimball's and buy a suit of clothes. We'll all be with you next Sunday.'

After the reconciliation, Father Scanlan called a meeting of the miners and asked for donations to build a hospital where the sick and injured of the camp might be cared for. He went around the following day soliciting aid, and in two months the hospital was open and ready to receive patients.

At that time Utah was officially classified as mission territory. Its capital, Salt Lake City, had not yet been established by the Pope as a diocese. Its pastoral care was entrusted to an apostolic administrator – in this case the archbishop of San Francisco – who governed it in the name of the supreme pontiff. Furthermore, seventy percent of the population of the city and the state belonged to the Church of Jesus Christ of the Latter Day Saints, whose members were nicknamed Mormons.

The pioneer priests who ministered in this vast territory, which comprised 85,000 square miles and included a large portion of Nevada, were few and far between, and in many instances their morale was low. They and their flocks were like sheep without a shepherd. Archbishop Alemany, in his search for a charismatic figure to lead the far-off mission, sent for the young Tipperary priest and appointed him pastor of what must have been the largest parish in Christendom.

The long trek to the Mormon Mecca was arduous, tedious and lonely. It was a new beginning for the young priest, who was cut off not just from home and family but from the fraternal and supportive company of his fellow priests in San Francisco. He had been just five years a priest, administering the 85,000 square miles embraced by his parish alone, when a small band of priests, among whom was Denis Kiely, later his vicar-general, arrived. From the outset, Scanlan was a young man in a hurry. He traversed the entire territory, laying the foundations for almost every parish in what would later become a diocese. He built more than thirty churches, established schools and hospitals and left flourishing Christian communities in his wake. The picture that emerges is someone very solid, substantial and energetic, covering prodigious distances on horseback, coach, and train – staying sometimes for longer or shorter periods with one of other of his communities, but mostly on the move.

His real work, of course, was telling everyone who would listen to him about the birth, ministry, death and resurrection of Jesus Christ. It was a constant source of wonder how Scanlan managed to cover the enormous mileage that he did in his lifetime. He was carrying a great light to shine in the darkness of a sick world – he was taking with him a new faith, a new hope, a new freedom.

Back in Salt Lake City he founded the College of All Hallows, operated by the Marist Fathers, in 1885. On 29 June 1887 he was consecrated titular bishop of Larandum and vicar apostolic of Utah and he was named first bishop of the newly created Diocese of Salt Lake City on 30 January 1891. The Church in Utah was now firmly established, thanks to the missionary bishop from Ballytarsna.

The bishop now set his sights on the erection of a cathedral in Salt Lake City: a cathedral that would be worthy of the future Metropolitan See of the Church in Utah; a cathedral that would be a *lux in tenebris* – a beacon in the darkness of false religion; a cathedral in the Romanesque style that would display the richness of the Christian heritage. He laid the foundation stone for this building in 1900 and contributions came pouring in, not least from the Mormons and the miners of Pioche. He invited Cardinal James Gibbons to dedicate the magnificent structure on 15 August 1909, and as recently as 1970 the Cathedral of Madeleine was placed on the National Register of Historic Sites.

By now, the bishop's health was giving cause for concern. An illness contracted at Hamilton on his way to Pioche in 1869 and later diagnosed as a severe case of mountain fever had far-reaching effects that proved to be life-long and contributed to the exhaustion and debility of his later years. But he continued to work as long as he could find enough inner strength to carry on. Finally, when he reached the biblical age of three score and ten, he decided to retire and resigned himself to the care of the Sisters of Holy Cross, whose hospital he had founded.

He carried with him to Holy Cross Hospital his most treasured possession, the episcopal ring given to him by Archbishop Croke of Cashel. Croke was not slow to recognise the singular greatness of his colleague and co-diocesan from Ballytarsna. He saw him as a late-nineteenth-century Escalante who had helped the Lord gather a people unto himself. In sending him the ring, the archbishop told him that he had worn it himself, as had his predecessors in Cashel for centuries, and he expressed the hope that the ring would be a symbol of the bond uniting the bishop's adopted diocese with the diocese of his birth.

One newspaper described the death of Bishop Lawrence Scanlan on 10 May 1915 by saying 'A mighty oak has fallen'. Croke's ring figured in the bishop's last hours. As Father Kiely prayed by his bedside, he was interrupted by the bishop lifting his finger for his episcopal ring. Feeling it slipped on by his faithful old friend, he became content to die. His interment was carried out with great solemnity and dignity. His remains rest in the crypt beneath the high altar of the cathedral he had brought into existence.

The Mormons honoured his passing as they honoured his living amongst them. One of the Twelve Apostles of the Latter Day Saints commented: 'I regard him a saintly man who has won the sincere love and respect of every man and woman in the State of Utah by the true godliness of his life.'

We leave the last word to the Lord: 'Happy are the dead who die in the faith of Christ! They may rest from their labours, for they take with them the record of their deeds' (Revelation 14:13).

On Friday 13 October, having said early Mass, I went up on deck and got my first glimpse of the Statue of Liberty and the awesome New York skyline. For Louis and me it was our first time stepping onto a foreign shore. We were greeted by my aunts Sarah and Molly and a lot of their friends, including a cousin, Frank Barrett from Ballinure, who with his wife, Rita, would be our hosts for almost two weeks. For me, the greatest thrill of all was meeting my aunts and being able to thank them personally for their kindness and generosity to me over the years. I saw a lot of them during our stay and we were deluged with invitations to visit their friends. We were taken to see all the sights of New York.

My aunt Margaret came up from Washington and brought me back with her. I stayed there with her son Bill, a doctor, and his wife, Kitty, and again was brought sightseeing in the nation's capital. I was taken to the Capitol, where I saw the Senate and the House of Representatives in session. Then I returned to New York by train; I was met by Louis and Frank Barrett and went with them to Gaelic Park to see a hurling match between Offaly and Galway.

Time flew, and soon we were on the train to Chicago, where another welcome awaited us, this time from my father's sister Aunt Margaret. Again for the first time I was introduced to a host of cousins and their friends. On Sunday 29 October around sixty of them gathered in my aunt's house for a farewell party. For the first time we felt really lonely, as we were leaving that night for Seattle and then to Vancouver in Canada to catch the ship that would take us on the final stage of our journey to New Zealand. John, a first cousin, took us to the station accompanied by my aunt. We said our goodbyes at Union Station and, as our train sped into the night on its two-day journey to the West Coast, we suddenly realised that from here to New Zealand we were on our own, not knowing a soul en route. We had a comfortable bedroom and our day was spent in the observation carriage at the end of the train admiring the scenery.

We arrived in Seattle at 7.30 am on 1 November – the

Feast of All Saints. A doctor and his wife whom we had met in the observation carriage had a car waiting for them and they drove us to the cathedral, where we said Mass and met Father John Ball from Louisburgh, County Mayo, who had been a fellow student with us in Maynooth. He took us sightseeing after breakfast and put us on the train to Vancouver at midday. On arriving in Vancouver at 5.30 pm we had our baggage transferred to the *RMS Aorangi,* the ship that would take us to Auckland in New Zealand. Then we looked up the Irish Christian Brothers, where we stayed the night. The brothers gave us a truly Irish welcome, although only two of them were Irish. We slept that night in the college infirmary.

On Thursday 2 November – All Souls Day – we were headed for the high seas again. Louis said his three Masses in the parish church and I said mine in the brothers' oratory. After breakfast we bade farewell to the brothers and took a cab to the *RMS Aorangi*. The *Aorangi* was an old ship not nearly as nice or as up-to-date as the *SS America.* During the war it was requisitioned as a troop carrier. It was now the only passenger ship sailing between America and Australia. Louis and I had considerable difficulty in getting reservations on it, and when we finally succeeded in doing so we didn't even get into the same cabin. Each of us had three non-Catholics as travelling companions. Also travelling with us was Dr Doody, Bishop of Armidale, Australia, who was returning from Rome; Father Mulhern, a priest from Sydney; and Father Charles, a Polish priest on his way to Sydney to look after Polish refugees.

The ship sailed from Vancouver at 9 am; its first port of

call was Victoria, about ninety miles away, which we reached at 6 pm. Then we were on our way again on a three-week trek across the Pacific.

On Wednesday 8 November we reached Hawaii. The weather was getting very warm – so much so that I nearly passed out with the heat whilst saying Mass. At 4 pm we caught our first glimpse of the Hawaiian Islands, and we sailed into Honolulu shortly after 6 pm. To get ashore, we had to go through customs formalities, which took us some time, but we also saw our first Hawaiian sunset, and it was glorious. The horizon presented a panorama of beautiful colours which were reflected by the sea. We decided to stay close to the ship that night and the two of us entered a restaurant by the wharf and had some cool drinks. We were very impressed by the courtesy and friendliness of the waitresses who garlanded us with leis. Next thing, we heard a gasp from the doorway. It was the Aussie priest Father Mulhern who had been passing by when he saw us. He strode over to our table and bellowed, 'For Christ's sake, get out of here. You're in the biggest whorehouse in the Pacific!' The two innocents at large ran back to the ship and thanked the Lord for their deliverance!

Next day Father Mulhern, Father Charles, Louis and I shared a taxi which took us all around the island. We visited Pearl Harbour and the nearby cemetery, where there were thousands of little white crosses to the memory of the American soldiers who had lost their lives in the Pacific during the Second World War.

Our departure from Honolulu will always be a cherished memory of mine. Most of the passengers had garlands of flowers round their necks. The Hawaiian band played native music for us and the girls sang and did the native hula. Then they played and sang 'Auld Lang Syne' as the *Aorangi* pulled out on the next stage of the journey to Fiji.

On Wednesday 15 November there was a beautiful sunset. As I watched it on the top deck, I was joined by Frank Simpson, a New Zealand journalist. He told me that we were now on the route which the famous Captain Bligh had taken after the mutiny on the *HMS Bounty.* He really brought the whole story to life with his wonderfully descriptive language.

At midday on Friday 17 November we arrived in Suva, the capital of the Fiji Islands. These islands were then under British rule and were mainly occupied by native Fijians and Indians. Fiji is currently reaping the whirlwind of ethnic tensions that were brewing when we visited.

The Fijians themselves are an open-hearted, innocent and generous people that one cannot help liking. They have a reputation for strict honesty. The Indians, on the other hand, are the go-ahead type, and many of them are cunning, ambitious and unscrupulous in their business dealings. They came to the islands in the beginning as labourers and now own practically all the property in Fiji. All the big businesses and white-collar jobs are in their hands, whereas the Fijians are in the poor settlements and fill all the menial positions. The Indians are doing their best to dominate all the islands and it is believed that the racial question here will cause friction in the future. *(This paragraph in my diary was written almost fifty years ago, and in retrospect it now sounds prophetic.)*

Next day we hired a taxi and went on a tour of the island. We stopped at a typical Fijian village. The place was swarming with children, who flocked around us looking for pennies. The Fijian huts were made of some sort of sticks and grass. We entered one of them and it was spotlessly clean. The floor was covered with homemade carpets and, sleeping on the floor covered by a mosquito net, was a little child. The man of the house got a youngster to climb a coconut tree for us. It was amazing to see the child scurrying up the trunk like a monkey and throwing coconuts down to us.

We sailed from Fiji at 3 pm. Next stop Auckland!

On Monday 20 November I spent a good part of the day packing. Louis and I received a radiogram from Archbishop McKeefry which read: 'Warm welcome to New Zealand. Best wishes.' We had our farewell dinner in the evening, after which we got our friends to autograph our menu.

For the past three weeks, straight across the narrow corridor from my cabin there had been four young Mormon missionaries, two of them coming to New Zealand, the others continuing on to Australia. There was little or no communication between us. In our studies in Maynooth we had not been told anything about the Mormons, the Jehovah's Witnesses or indeed any of the American-founded destructive cults that had been emerging since the end of the Second World War. But we had been told about the Monophysites and the Monothelites, and the Gnostics and the Arians, and all the dead heresies of the earlier centuries. Another sad *lacuna* in our training.

Tuesday 21 November was our last day on the ship. After breakfast we got our first glimpse of the islands off the coast of New Zealand. At 5 o'clock we docked at Auckland, and after a few brief formalities we went down the gangway and stepped onto New Zealand soil, to be welcomed by a number of priests, including Father Willie Wood of Cashel, whom we knew. He told us that Archbishop McKeefry had given us permission to stay on in Auckland for two weeks before proceeding to Wellington. We were then taken to Ponsonby, where the first Catholic mission in the city was established by Bishop Pompallier, a Frenchman, in 1843.

8

Land of the Long White Cloud

Ao-tea-roa – 'The Long White Cloud' – was the name the Maoris gave to New Zealand when they arrived there in their canoes. The Maoris are a branch of the Polynesian race that migrated to the Pacific Islands from Malaya or Indonesia, then spread out fanwise to colonise the scattered islands in Oceania. The land was renamed by the Dutch, its first European discoverers, 'Nieuw Zeeland', which was Anglicised to 'New Zealand' by Captain James Cook when he arrived in 1769. These lands were 'new' only to Europeans. They were old lands to the Maoris and other peoples who had lived in them from time immemorial.

New Zealand is an archipelago in the South Pacific consisting of two large islands – North Island, which covers 44,281 square miles, and South Island, with an area of 58,093 square miles – and a number of smaller islands near the coasts. The British crown formally annexed the land of the Maoris in 1788 but active British colonisation did not begin until 1840.

As more white settlers arrived, the Maoris regretted the treaties they had signed with the Europeans. They considered that they had been tricked out of their ancestral heritage. From 1840 to 1870 the Maoris conducted a series of wars against the *pakehas* ('whites'). Although they were defeated, they won peace with honour.

The city of Auckland with a population of just over 300,000 in 1950, is the largest city in New Zealand, although

Wellington is the capital of the country. Auckland is situated on an isthmus facing two oceans, the Tasman Sea on one side and the Pacific Ocean on the other. The isthmus is hilly, with seven peaks, the highest being Mount Eden and One Tree Hill.

It was providential that our sojourn in New Zealand should begin in Ponsonby, not least because of that town's association with Jean Baptiste Francois Pompallier, Auckland's first bishop. Pompallier was a man of God with little or no understanding of the things of Mammon. He was forever up to his eyes in debt because of poor investments in land and reckless spending on a palatial residence for himself called Mount St Mary's. In 1868 he declared himself bankrupt and was forced to sell or mortgage much of the diocesan church property. Finally, his own house and personal belongings were seized.

There were also serious pastoral problems: the majority of the priests were still French, although the colony was British and there was a great influx of Irish, many of them attracted by the lure of gold in Thames. The double barrier of race and language was proving to be an insuperable obstacle to the spread of the faith in the country. Eventually Pompallier resigned and returned to France. His successor, Thomas W. Croke, later to become Archbishop of Cashel, was appointed and consecrated Bishop of Auckland in the Church of St Agatha in Rome. He then left for New Zealand on the understanding that his mandate was to put the Church there back on its feet. This he did, even to extent that he repurchased Mount St Mary's as the official residence of the bishop.

There was an added bonus in being in Ponsonby in

those days. All of the four priests in Ponsonby parish were Irish; two of them, Willie Wood and Phil Purcell, were with us during our year in St Patrick's College, Thurles. John Daly, one of the priests who met us on our arrival, was from Kerry, and the administrator, Monsignor Kennedy, was a Wexford man, very quiet and reserved but exceedingly nice. Being in this company for two weeks was an enriching pastoral experience and a wonderful preparation for what lay before us in Wellington. In the evenings Irish priests from the city parishes would call over to greet us and enquire about the homeland. Some of them had not seen their families for ten years: the only way of getting home was by sea, and that was slow and expensive. Often they had to sell their cars to make up the fare. Before the age of air mail and air travel, the sender of a letter would have to wait at least three months for a reply, so relatively fresh news from home was always welcome. One fellow Tipperary man, Father Bill Doherty of Avondale, brought along an old *Irish Catholic Directory* and called out a list of his own contemporaries, enquiring after each one in turn. Pen in hand, he made the necessary annotations, and each deletion was accompanied by 'May the Lord have mercy on him'. When the litany of invocations for the dead ended, Bill closed the book, shook his head slowly and sighed, 'Well, there are not many of us left. The Light of Heaven to them all.'

An unforgettable character was the genial Johnny O'Connor, a Kerryman in the mould of Jeremiah the Prophet, who dropped some pastoral pearls into our laps. Amongst his more quotable quotes: 'Read, lads, read, and keep up your reading, because if you don't read you can't feckin' well preach.' And again, this time on pastoral visitation: *'Cognoscere oves,* lads ... know the sheep if you want to be a good shepherd ... and you'll never get to know them unless you visit them in their homes ... a house-going priest makes a church-going people.' These words of wisdom scorched themselves into my memory almost half a century ago and have been with me ever since.

Before leaving for Wellington, another treat lay in store for us. During our stop-over in Fiji we were told that twenty-four young Irish girls had called to the island just over a year previously en route to Auckland to enter the Sisters of Mercy. They were a happy, carefree group who sang Irish songs and danced jigs and reels to the music of an accordion on the streets of Suva. The Fijians took them to their hearts and, before boarding the ship for the last stage of the journey, they were garlanded with flowers. We were told that they were now in the novitiate of St Mary's Convent, right on our doorstep here in Ponsonby. Meeting them was an unforgettable experience. They were sitting, all twenty-four of them, around a long table in the community hall, and we were greeted with a chorus of *'Cead Míle Fáilte'*. It was a moving sight to behold so many young Irish girls at such a tender age leaving home and family – possibly never to return – to witness to Christ in such a far-off land. It was an afternoon of music and song in which all of us joined, and when I mentioned the lovely memories that they left behind them in Suva, one of them whispered to me, 'Don't breathe a word of this to the Mistress of Novices. Before leaving Fiji we all had our hair done. For the last time!' she added, poignantly.

This was a unique experience that would never be repeated and would be totally incomprehensible in the light of today's virtual extinction of the sisterhood. A couple of years later Louis, myself and three confrères piled into a small car and made the long, tortuous journey – over 900 miles there and back! – from Wellington to Auckland for the girls' First Profession. The *Cead Míle Fáilte*'s had an extra fervour this time. Our presence meant a lot to them.

Our own Auckland novitiate ended on the evening of 4 December, when we boarded the train for the fourteen-hour journey to Wellington. We had a bedroom all to ourselves and lost no time in getting some rest. On awaking, we had our first opportunity of viewing the terrain through which we were passing. It was bathed in brilliant sunshine and was rugged and beautiful.

Wellington in 1950 was celebrating just one hundred years of Catholicism. This was a culture shock for the two of us, coming as we were from a country with a Christian heritage of over 1,500 years. Bishop Philip Viard, a Frenchman, arrived in Wellington on the barque *Clara* on 1 May 1850. With him were five Marist priests – six more would arrive from Auckland in the following months. The town's population at the time was about 5,000, and the Catholic people gave them a very warm welcome. This was the event which brought the diocese of Wellington into existence. During his first decade in the diocese, which extended from Taupo in the middle of the North Island down to Bluff at the lower extremity of the South Island, Bishop Viard had to service this vast area with only nine priests.

Earthquakes shook the capital city throughout 1855, starting in January and continuing until December. Bishop Viard got his people praying and, as the feast of the Imma-

My home – the Post Office in Ballinure

Pake Kirwan [above] *and*
Willie Duggan [right]
who left cherished memories

Putting the Postal Service on Wheels
Back: [l] *Paddy Donnelly and* [r] *Jack Power*
Front: [l] *Willie Duggan and* [r] *Anthony Power*

Ordination Day, 18 June 1950
[l. to r.] *James Feehan, Gus McCauley, Maynooth President, Mons. Edward Kissane, Vincent Morris and Louis Gleeson*

Maynooth Professor, Walter McDonald whose sole desire was to tell the truth

Lawrence Scanlan
A model bishop

Cardinal Peter McKeefrey
Prince among Archbishops

Bill Heavey – my first pastor

Jimmy Houlihan – moving the earth in the cause of fraternity

Bill Walsh and Louis Gleeson – bound for the Elysian fields

Charles Bianconi – king of the Irish roads

James Meehan [below] *man of God and champion of the poor*

The Carre family – beatitudes from the Captain Cook

Bulfins, the last thatched house, restored by the present owner Roger Condon

'Tis all chequerboard of Nights and Days
Where destiny with Men of Pieces plays
Rubaiyat of Omar Khyyam
(photo: Sinéad Ní Riain)

culate Conception approached, he prepared for a Solemn Triduum. Hundreds attended the Triduum, and after 8 December the last of the tremors died away.

The discovery of gold in the late 1850s went on to bring not only economic benefits to Bishop Viard's diocese but an immigration of thousands of Irish miners and their families to increase its Catholic population. As a result of the Gold Rush, the expansion of the Church on the west coast was rapid. Irish priests followed the thousands of miners and their families to the diggings. This was a period of rapid expansion: churches were built all over the South Island, and in time the dioceses of Christchurch and Dunedin detached themselves from Wellington.

In 1868 Bishop Viard went to Rome to report on the state of his diocese. There he met the young Father Francis Redwood, SM, and asked for him as a coadjutor bishop. Viard died on 2 June 1872, to be succeeded by Bishop Redwood, who at thirty-four was then the youngest bishop in the world. When he died, sixty-one years later, he was the oldest. He immediately swung into action, establishing parishes in many parts of the diocese: Mount Victoria, where I would spend my entire time in Wellington, was founded in 1913, and Kilbirnie, just five minutes away, where Louis would minister, was founded in 1919.

When Archbishop Redwood died on 3 January 1935, Wellington was an archdiocese that had been in existence for eighty-five years. He was succeeded by Archbishop O'Shea, another Marist. He had as his coadjutor Peter McKeefry, who would shortly succeed him and under whom we would be privileged to serve for the next five years.

As our train sped towards the capital city on that sunny

summer's morning, Louis and I reflected on some of the things we had learned during our stay in Auckland. The Secular Education Act of 1876 had been passed despite the active opposition of Archbishop Redwood and Dunedin's first bishop, the Irishman Dr Moran. This meant that, if Catholics wanted their own schools, they would have to build, staff and maintain them at their own expense as well as paying taxes towards the State's secular system. Undaunted, Redwood brought religious teaching orders from Australia, England and Ireland. The expansion of schools and convents he achieved was breathtaking. He received great support from the laity in financing this development and his endeavours were continued by his successors, particularly Peter McKeefry, who coaxed and cajoled every teaching order in Ireland to make new foundations in New Zealand. He even persuaded Dom. Celsus O'Connell, Lord Abbot of Mount Melleray, to establish the first ever Cistercian monastery in the Southern Hemisphere, in the Archdiocese of Wellington.

Our train arrived at Wellington at 9.40 am on Tuesday 5 December 1950. Waiting for us on the platform were Gerry Timoney, who had been ordained in Maynooth in 1947 and was on loan from his home diocese of Clogher; Tom Hennebry from Mooncoin; and Hughie McHale from Dublin. There was no concelebration in those days, so we went to different parishes to celebrate Mass. Gerry brought me to Archbishop O'Shea's residence, where I said my first Mass in Wellington. The archbishop, now in his eighties, was in hospital. His house served as presbytery to four priests in St Joseph's parish, Mount Victoria. After Mass we went to St

Anne's, Newtown, where Louis had celebrated Mass. There we met two of the great senior pioneering priests of the archdiocese, Monsignor John Kelly from Mullinavat and Monsignor James McManus from Leitrim, from whom we garnered pastoral wisdom at its richest and best.

I had never administered the last rites or even seen a person die. When I mentioned this, John Kelly straightaway reassured me by recreating memories of his first anointing, way back in the 1890s. The recipient was his first parish priest, a pioneering giant who rode horseback into the native settlements, evangelising the Maoris. His recreation was to travel into the hills with his gun and dog in pursuit of wildlife. 'The great man could see that I was nervous,' mused John, 'so after I had struggled through the rite and asked if there was anything else I could do for him, he looked at me with a mischievous glint in his eye. "There is, John," said he. "When I'm put in the coffin, would you ever put the auld gun in along with me. 'Cause you'd never know, John," he continued, "I might get an auld shot when I'm goin' through the Valley of Jehosophat!" I was never nervous again after that.'

Monsignor McManus was another trail-blazer for Christ. The stories of his pastoral and missionary experiences were awe-inspiring. He was parish priest of Palmerston North, where he built a magnificent church dedicated to St Patrick. It is now the cathedral church of the new diocese of Palmerston North, a fitting monument to his memory.

We were taken to an annual sports day for the Catholic schools of the city. It was organised by the clergy, so the event was an opportunity for us to meet the priests of the city: needless to say, many of them were Irish. We also met the sisters, who, like the priests, were unashamedly partisan where their own schools were concerned. Archbishop McKeefry arrived in the afternoon to present the prizes and was immediately surrounded by hundreds of children. He gave Louis and myself a heart-warming welcome and told us to take a few days' rest before settling down to work. Both of us stayed at St Joseph's, where Monsignor Bill Heavey was pastor and Gerry Timoney curate. Here we met the chancellor, Monsignor Jock McRae, whose offices were in the building. He is, I believe, the tallest priest in the world – seven feet and a few inches. Louis was to become his curate and it was a constant source of amusement to all of us to see Louis, a six-footer himself, having to look up at his pastor when conversing with him.

A week later six Irish priests, newly ordained like ourselves, arrived in Wellington. They were for permanent service in the archdiocese. Louis and I went down to the wharf to meet them and a large gathering of priests, including the archbishop, greeted them as they came down the gangway. For them it was their first taste of the wonderful fraternity that was so much a hallmark of the New Zealand Church. Appointments followed a week later. Louis was sent to Kilbirnie and I was appointed to St Joseph's, with Bill Heavey as my pastor and Gerry Timoney my colleague.

Bill came to Wellington with his brother Bert from the southern province of Otago. They found themselves lodgings with three other South Islanders in a boarding house run by an Irish landlady. Bill was forever praising the faith and wholesome Christian values of this remarkable woman. And well he might, because all five of them returned to Otago and entered the national seminary in Mosgiel to study for the priesthood. All were ordained, three of them for priestly service in the South Island. Bill and Bert Heavey could have chosen their own diocese of Dunedin as the scene of their future ministry, but because of the inspirational influence and encouragement of their erstwhile hostess they opted instead to serve the Lord in the Metropolitan See of Wellington. And what a stroke of Divine Providence it was that Bill should be my first pastor and Gerry my associate. Gerry was the one who first encouraged me 'to get out and meet the people'. He literally wore out his shoe leather as he trudged the hilly streets of Mount Victoria on house visits.

The presbytery in Paterson Street was a haven of hospitality. There were three spare rooms and it was open house for priests visiting the city or in transit to the South Island, so we were never short of company. Besides, Louis was only five minutes away through a nearby road tunnel, so we were constantly toing and froing. On Sunday nights we went to the Irish Club, where we cemented new friendships to the sound of music and laughter.

Strangely, I was never lonely in Paterson Street. After a few weeks Gerry went on his holidays and Bill, thinking that I was going through the pangs of loneliness, insisted one evening on taking me to the pictures. 'It has an Irish flavour about it,' he said. 'It's called *Abie's Irish Rose.'* The film itself was pure schmaltz but the occasion was a memorable one. We were waiting at the tram stop when a car drove up and the driver called, 'Where to, Monsignor?'

'The Plaza, please,' replied Bill, as we took our seats.

On arrival at the cinema, Bill was about to purchase the tickets when another voice called, 'Allow me, Monsignor', and handed us our tickets.

The surprises weren't over yet, as a lady then came and offered us a box of chocolates 'to chew during the show'. Inside, Bill opened the box of Black Magic and handed it to me with the wry comment, 'Now, won't it be just too bad if we don't get a ride home?'

What I loved about the work at St Joseph's was its seemingly infinite variety: home and hospital visits, instructing prospective converts to the faith, Catholic Youth Movement activities, religious instruction in the schools and visiting the prison. The governor and his deputy were excellent Catholics, so we had free access to the prisoners' cells; here too were formed firm friendships with the most unlikely characters.

The prevailing atmosphere in the city was one of indifference to religion. Catholics constituted only one in seven of the population, and the majority of these were actively involved in their church but were surrounded by a sea of indifference, which inevitably took its toll. The church in St Joseph's was a wooden structure, as was the one in Louis' parish Kilbirnie.

At the end of the first year Gerry was moved to Palmerston North, and in his place came a newly ordained priest of Irish parentage. His name was Billy Walsh and he had Hodgkin's disease, a chronic malignant disease of the lymphatic tissues. He was given two years to live, and from the time he came to Paterson Street he was a young man in a hurry. My two years with him were the most precious experience of my entire priesthood. In my student days and often during my first year in the priesthood I asked myself, 'What would you do if you knew exactly when you were going to die? How would you live your life?' The Lord answered my query in the truly wonderful experience of living with and observing the life of Bill Walsh.

Shortly after his arrival, Bishop Hugh O'Neill of Dunedin came to live with us. He resigned as coadjutor bishop of the southern diocese as a result of a mild stroke and, so as not to embarrass his successor by staying on, decided to come to Paterson Street at the invitation of Archbishop McKeefry. Around the same time we had another newcomer in the person of Mattie Kolich, a Croatian priest who had two doctorates and was fluent in five languages. Mattie was intensely proud of his Croatian nationality and was highly insulted whenever he was described as a Yugoslav. He just smiled benignly, however, when Bishop O'Neill called him a Bulgarian, because to the bishop all east Europeans were classified as Bulgarians. There was a sizeable Croatian community in Wellington, not all of them churchgoers. One day during lunch we were discussing what happens after death. This led to a difference of opinion between Mattie and the bishop on the issue of judgement, at which point Bill Walsh joined us at the table.

'Bill, will you for God's sake talk to this bloody Bulgarian. I can't get him to see the light,' groaned the exasperated bishop.

'What's this all about?' queried Bill.

'It is about the judgement after death,' sighed the Croatian.

Bill immediately diffused the situation with one of his inimitable shafts of humour. Putting his arm around Mattie's shoulders, he commented good-naturedly, 'Ah yes, Mattie, that's the day that the good Lord will separate the sheep from the Croats!'

Recalling the incident later, Mattie said to me, 'How could I possibly take offence at what Bill said? The man is full of the joy of the Spirit and this was just a fresh effusion of it.' How right he was. That was my first lesson from the life of Bill Walsh – joy and happiness in the Spirit of the Lord.

My second memory of Bill is the amount of work he got through daily, not merely in visiting homes, classrooms and hospitals, but in the hours he spent in Mount Crawford prison, sitting in cells with prisoners of all denominations, listening to them and giving them hope. Where did the strength come from for all this activity? He found the answers in Mark 6:46: 'He bade them farewell and then withdrew into the hills to pray.' Bill's hill was the oratory in Paterson Street on Mount Victoria, where he spent hours alone with the Lord. Withdrawal with God gave him peace within and a serenity that was infectious to others. I believe that it was in this area that he most resembled the Lord. There was a rhythm about the life of Jesus – withdrawal and work, withdrawal and work – which he sought to teach his apostles. He didn't have to teach it to Bill.

Another of my memories of Bill must also be told. Bill Heavey had one abiding problem – a property adjacent to the church which had a bad name because of the nightly shenanigans that went on there. Even more important, he badly needed it for parish purposes. The asking price was £50,000, or the equivalent of half a million pounds today. The chancellor, Monsignor McRae, laughed derisively when asked for a loan. Bill Walsh and I normally went to Athletic Park on Saturday to watch the rugby. One Saturday, however, he decided to give the football a miss, so I went off on my own. On my return, he came into my room in a state of great excitement. This is what he said to me.

'I was on my own in the presbytery when the doorbell rang and this elderly gentleman said he wanted to talk to a priest. He was in an unholy mess – hadn't been to the church for almost forty years. There's lots more, but my lips are sealed. Anyway, I can recognise true repentance when I see it, and this was the real thing. I gave him absolution and you should have seen the sense of relief that simply flowed over him.

'We chatted on for a while and then he said that he'd like to do something worthwhile for the Church. Was there anything that the parish needed?

'I suddenly thought of Monsignor Heavey's dream and told him about it. "How much will it cost?" he asked.

'"Fifty thousand," I gulped.

'There and then he took out his chequebook and handed me a cheque for that amount. I couldn't believe my eyes. Now just watch Bill Heavey's face when I hand this to him at tea.'

At tea that evening Bill drew down the subject casually, saying, 'That den of iniquity down at the Basin Reserve, Monsignor, are you still anxious to have it?'

'Of course I am, but I've given up all hope. You might as well try getting blood out of a turnip as getting anything from old Jock McRae.'

'Perhaps this might be of some help,' said Bill, placing the cheque in front of the Monsignor.

Bill Heavey nearly had apoplexy. 'Is this genuine?' he eventually spluttered.

'Of course it is,' Bill assured him. 'The Lord specially

planned this by getting me to stay away from the rugby match today.' Then he told the story again.

On Monday morning Bill Heavey bought the house of ill-repute and, like the Ethiopian in the Scriptures, went on his way rejoicing. And the cause of his joy? The little man from Taranaki whose days were now numbered.

The doctors were right. His priesthood lasted two years almost to the day. I said Mass in his hospital room the morning that he died and gave him the Sacrament of the Sick.

'Is there anything else I can do for you Bill?' I asked.

'There is, Jim.' The words came with an effort. 'Pray with me. Because I can't think and I can't pray.'

My God, I thought, here is a man who knew he was going to die and prepared for this hour by a life of prayer ... and now he can't pray. What hope is there for me? Bill did not need to pray because his life was a prayer, and when the end came it too was a living prayer.

The church was full to overflowing for his Requiem. They came from every walk of life, amongst them six men in prison garb accompanied by a few officers. Peter McKeefry had considerable difficulty in controlling his emotions during his panegyric and then, as he concluded the prayer of final farewell, there was a sudden commotion in the church. Archbishop and congregation looked on in amazement as the prisoners were seen to bolt from their seats. It was not an escape bid; they made straight for the casket, which they lifted and carried shoulder-high down the church. The congregation looked on transfixed. Nothing like this had ever been seen before, and I dare say nothing like it has ever been seen since.

Paterson Street, especially when Monsignor Bill Heavey was pastor, gave me a wonderful opportunity to meet the other New Zealand bishops, especially Bishop John Kavanagh of Dunedin, who was a frequent visitor, as it was from Paterson Street that he was appointed to the southern diocese. Bishops from Australia and the islands of Oceania also stayed with us when visiting the capital city, so I got to know many of them. But for me the prelate who influenced my life more than any other in my entire priesthood was Peter McKeefry, archbishop of Wellington, primate of New Zealand and the first cardinal in the history of the New Zealand Church. He was editor of *Zealandia,* the Catholic newspaper, when he was appointed successor to Archbishop O'Shea.

He was a priest of the diocese of Auckland and he told me that it was with some trepidation that he came south to take over the Metropolitan See. The clergy of Wellington would have preferred one of their own, and in particular John Kavanagh, who later became Bishop of Dunedin. But from the time Peter McKeefry arrived amongst them, with two suitcases containing all his worldly possessions, they took him to their hearts. He was over six feet tall, lean, restless and full of nervous energy; a man of touching humility, with no interest in the trappings of his high office. He wore his cardinal's robes reluctantly and only on important ceremonial occasions, preferring the plain cassock of a parish priest. All he owned was a record player, some records and a stack of books. He lived in just two rooms in a busy city presbytery.

Shortly after our arrival, he brought the eight young Irish priests together to give us our appointments. The advice that he gave us on that summer's morning is still fresh with me. He put fraternity at the top of the list of the things vital to priestly life, telling us that it seemed to him that fraternity was the proper way of living celibacy; that it would be tragic if we concluded that the vocation to be celibate was a vocation to be solitary, withdrawn and unrelated. And then, as we were to discover, the practical warning that to live in fraternity does not mean that we would always agree; life would be very dull if we did. Noticing that all of us were wearing pioneer pins, he had this to say: 'I'm glad to see you wearing the pin. For me, temperance is a virtue, whereas total abstinence isn't. If in the future you do decide to take a drink, just remember two things: never, ever on your own and never, ever before midday – advice that has stood to me down the years.'

Some years later, as he was seated at his desk, talking on the phone to one of his priests, death came suddenly and unexpectedly to Peter Cardinal McKeefry. While he lived, he wrote a last will, which was read at his Requiem Mass. It was extremely simple. It consisted of just one sentence: 'I declare myself to be possessed of no property, real or personal.'

Monsignor Bill Heavey was soon to follow him – and has earned himself a place in the clerical lore of New Zealand as the priest who preached at his own funeral. In his last years, Bill was wont to philosophise on the vicissitudes of life. One evening he discoursed on the Last Things with his pastor, Tim Hannigan. Tim was so impressed with Bill's preparation for death and his firm faith in the pledge of eternal life given by Christ himself in John, chapter six, that he surreptitiously recorded the conversation and played it back in the homily at Bill's funeral mass. 'I'll just let the monsignor speak for himself,' he said, before switching on the tape. The people sat enchanted and spellbound as, even in death, the words of wisdom flowed once again from the priest they had known and loved so well.

I had left New Zealand when Bill Heavey delivered his posthumous homily, but from my notes and recollections of my first pastor and mentor I have a fair idea of what he may have said. He would surely have included the following pearls, which he shared with me.

'On the day we die, all our pounds will be devalued – 100%.

'Across the final frontier we take nothing with us, only the treasures resulting from our being salt and light. We risk no devaluation with these.'

Christ's words to Martha on the death of her brother (John 11:21–27) were an integral part of his funeral homilies and reflections on his own death. 'My God, Jimmy,' he would say, 'listen to what he said to that girl in her tears: "Your brother will rise again! How do I know? Because I am the Resurrection and the Life! The one who lives and believes in me will never die." Then he said to her, "Do you believe this?"

'A question we'll all have to answer. I believe it, and I believe and know that, when my turn comes, I'll be leaving the land of the dying and heading for the land of the living.'

Besides his inspirational example, I owe an eternal debt to Bill for introducing me to Tom Fahey, who, like himself, was of good Irish stock from central Otago. Early in 1951 he came to Paterson Street and made it his base when promoting the Catholic newspaper the *New Zealand Tablet* in the archdiocese of Wellington. For close on fifty years, Tom has enriched my life by being my Anam Cara in the truest sense of the term. In him, throughout the longest and most abiding friendship of my priesthood, I have experienced all the riches of wisdom and knowledge that Paul speaks about (1 Corinthians 12:8). He is happily still with us, living in retirement in Dunedin.

Thanks, Tom, for the memories. *Ad multos annos!*

9

Bigotry and Beatitude

At the Edinburgh International Festival last year, the young composer James McMillan denounced his country as a land of 'sleepwalking bigotry' and 'visceral anti-Catholicism'. And, apropos of the Reformation obscurantism in the field of art and music, he remarked that 'one could draw interesting parallels between Mao Tse-tung and John Knox, Pol Pot and Andrew Melville' – insulting references to the founders of Scottish Presbyterianism. In the furore that followed the writer Andrew O'Hagan spoke of the birds in the trees singing sectarian songs in the west of Scotland and a professor of English eloquently denounced the folk culture that encompasses the sectarian songs sung by Rangers fans at Old Firm soccer matches.

Midway during my term in New Zealand I was given a unique chance to observe Scottish bigotry and sectarianism at close quarters. Once again I found myself on an ocean liner – for ten weeks, no less, plying between Wellington and Glasgow. It was a Scottish ship, renamed the *Captain Cook* because of its function in transporting skilled labour from the home countries to New Zealand. In the 1950s each year it carried 6,000 members of the trades and professions with their partners and families to a new life beneath the Southern Cross, free, gratis and for nothing, courtesy of the New Zealand government. Each voyage took 1,500 passengers from the port of Glasgow and lasted three months: five weeks to Wellington via the Panama Canal, then, having disembarked its passengers, five weeks back to Glasgow. Then, after a fortnight's break, it set out again with a further assortment of new immigrants.

Thanks to Archbishop McKeefry, I was appointed Catholic chaplain to one of these trips. When I embarked on the *Captain Cook* at the end of August 1953 I was one of just three passengers, my travelling companions being an Anglican clergyman and a Scottish Presbyterian doctor. We were the proverbial Irishman, Englishman and Scotsman, with a crew of 800 to look after us! As we sailed out of Wellington, I soon realised that I was the only Catholic on the ship's main deck. All the officers were Protestants. One could palpably sense the cold Calvinism from them. Despite the request of the New Zealand government that chaplains be afforded officer status, I was made to feel from the outset that I was just not one of them; that my services were irrelevant on the homeward journey and appertained only to those who would embark in Glasgow. My services were certainly irrelevant on the main deck, where I was in a minority of one, but my predecessor on the last trip had forewarned me that there was plenty of scope for pastoral work amongst the crew on the lower deck.

With just three passengers on the main deck, I was never invited to the captain's table at dinner – a courtesy that was normal on all sea-going voyages. Jimmy McMurren, the head barman, was the highest-ranking Catholic on board. He briefed me on the situation that one had to be a member of the Masonic or Orange Lodges to have any prospects of promotion on this shipping line. Jimmy was the person who introduced me to the sectarianism that was Scotland's shame.

'If you want to meet some Catholics, Father, I'll take you

down to the galleys, as we call them, but even these are outnumbered by Rangers supporters, and Father, I may as well tell you, *they're* a bad lot. You'll hear them singing "The Sash" and "Kick the Pope", but never mind – there are plenty of Celtic supporters too to belt out a few bars of "The Soldier's Song".'

Being a Glasgow ship, the religious divide was not so much Protestant versus Catholic as Rangers versus Celtic. I visited all the Celtic supporters in their crowded quarters on the lower deck and arranged Masses and Confessions for them. I listened to the exploits of Cheekie Charlie, Charlie Tully – 'Ireland's gift to Scotland'. I was told how in a Scottish Cup Final against the auld enemy, Charlie scored what should have been the winning goal direct from a corner kick but had to take it again, as the ref had not blown his whistle.

Charlie obliged by again turning the ball into the Rangers net, for which he was first mobbed by the ecstatic Celtic following, then canonised and ultimately deified. Next day the Celtic manager found him in a queue for sausages at a butcher's stall (due to post-war rationing). Feeling that this was beneath the dignity of the newly crowned King of Parkhead, he willingly offered to take Charlie's place in the queue. There he was spotted by the Ranger manager, who happened to be passing and asked him what he was doing.

'I'm getting a pound of sausages for Charlie Tully.'

'And you're getting a bloody good bargain, at that,' said the Rangers supremo as he went on his way, still licking his wounds.

Another story had a ticketless Celtic fan of low stature outside Ibrox for the Old Firm derby. Hearing a cheer inside, he asked a disgruntled Rangers trio watching the game from a high wall, 'What's happening? What's happening?'

'Och,' one of them said, 'there's been a fracas and ten Celtic Fenians got red cards. There's only Charlie Tully left.'

Shortly afterwards there was again thunderous applause within. 'What's happening now?' asked the little Celtic fan. 'Tell me, did Charlie score?'

In contrast with the cold Calvinists upstairs, the Catholic crewmen on the lower deck were a loveable, warm-hearted bunch. They came to me with their problems and told me about their sweethearts and families and how they were longing to be reunited with their loved ones. One memory from that time that has stayed with me down the years is of a young man who came to me in great distress. He told me about his girlfriend, who had been received into the Catholic Church shortly before he left on this trip and whom he hoped to marry before the end of the year. But then he had received disturbing news from home in a letter, which had awaited him in Curaçao, where the ship had docked to refuel. In this letter, it was broken to him by his mother that Barbara, his girlfriend, had been seen recently wearing a Rangers scarf in, of all places, Parkhead – the citadel of Celtic. 'Father,' he sighed, 'she couldna be a good Catholic and do that to me!' But love conquers all. I did my best to allay his fears.

I discovered too on the lower deck that bigotry can be a two-way street, as in the description of Scottish Orangemen as 'in-bred lumpen scum' and the definition of a Rangers fan (given by a Celtic supporter, of course) as a man who would marry a prostitute and then drag her down to his own level!

Our trip took us by Pitcairn Island in the south-west Pacific. The island was, of course, made famous by Fletcher Christian, ringleader of the mutiny against Captain William Bligh of the *Bounty* in 1789. Bligh and eighteen of his men were cast adrift in an open boat with little food and no chart, but after a marathon journey of 4,000 miles they reached Timor in the East Indies. Christian and eight other mutineers took refuge on Pitcairn Island, where they burned the *Bounty* and founded a settlement. Our boat made a brief stop off Pitcairn and the islanders came out in their boats, selling souvenirs. I bought a nice carved walking stick, which I still have. The vendor told me his name was Christian – he was no doubt descended from Fletcher. We then passed through the Panama Canal and refuelled in Curaçao. Then we sailed across the Atlantic and docked in Glasgow after five weeks on the high seas. On disembarking, I flew home to Ireland and had barely two weeks with my family. It was truly wonderful to see my parents and family again, even though it was such a short stop-over.

It was the beginning of October 1953 when I re-embarked on the *Captain Cook* for the long trek back to New Zealand. What a difference there was between the two journeys! The Masonic oligarchy that ruled the roost on the homeward voyage was swamped on the way back by a new tide of humanity – the 1,500 people who aimed to carve out a new life for themselves in a new country at the far end of the earth. As the ship was sailing down the Clyde, two young people came to me and introduced themselves as Jimmy Forkin from Roscommon and Sheila Hope from Belfast. They had been active members of the Legion of Mary at home. They now offered to round up the Catholics on board and asked if they might have the use of my cabin to say the Rosary during October. I agreed, and the two packed them in like sardines, and still they came. Most of them were young Irish men and women who had been working in England and were thus entitled to avail of the free passage to New Zealand.

On the first Sunday at sea they packed the lounge for Mass. I welcomed them and arranged a few get-togethers where I could give them the benefit of my limited experience in the land that would shortly be adopting them. I announced Confessions and got more than I had bargained for. Jimmy Forkin and some of his accomplices rounded up a few backsliders and press-ganged them into repentance! Catholic action at its ebullient best.

As each grace-filled day followed its predecessor, I began to wonder more and more at the things that had upset me on the homeward voyage, like not having been invited to sit at the captain's table! Yet here I was morning after morning at the Lord's table watching these faith-filled people partaking of the Bread of Life at my invitation. In the five weeks of the voyage, during which we traversed two oceans, the Atlantic and Pacific, I got to know many of my travelling companions, Catholic and non-Catholic. Each of them had a story to tell of hopes and expectations of what lay before them in the Land of the Long White Cloud.

One morning shortly after passing through the Panama Canal, as I was saying Mass in the lounge, I sensed a new presence in the congregation. It was Iris, a non-Catholic from Jersey in the Channel Islands who was travelling with her husband, Frank Carre, and two small children, Francis and Angela. I was surprised to see her at Mass, as on my first introduction to her she had politely given me the cold shoulder. Yet here she was sitting beside Sheila, both reading from the same missal. I said a quiet prayer to the Lord, asking him to give her a gentle fall from her high horse, just as he had done for St Paul. That evening she called to my cabin for a chat before dinner.

'You know,' she began, 'I was at your service this morning.' I nodded, and she went on, 'The strangest thing happened to me. I sensed another presence beside you, tangible and real – so real that I had to return to my cabin to recover from the experience.' I explained to her that there was indeed another presence – the Lord's – that it was a real presence and that she had truly been in the presence of the Divine.

'I'd like to find out a bit more about what you believe,' she continued. 'Now don't jump to any conclusions. It's too early for that. You see, until I came aboard this ship I had never in my life encountered a good Catholic. Those I met here have been a revelation. All I can say is: if the faith means so much to Jimmy and Sheila, well I'd like to know some more about it.'

So we arranged that she would come for half an hour's instruction every evening before dinner. Prayer was her first priority, so we began each session with a prayer. She showed a genuine spirit of enquiry, asked searching questions, and soon had a mature grasp of the truths contained in the Apostles' Creed. We went on then to the Sacraments, giving special attention to the Eucharist. She came in one evening bubbling with excitement and, after the opening prayer, she blurted out, 'I've decided, I'm going to go the whole way. I'm going to be a Catholic!'

I closed my eyes and said a few silent Alleluias. 'Now,' she added, 'Frank will have to pull his socks up.'

'I'll see to that,' I assured her, but there was no need. Frank was part of the general rejoicing amongst the Irish when the good news percolated through during dinner. The instructions continued until the ship arrived in Wellington and tied up in the harbour, just a stone's throw from the city centre. It was night, and the mirrorlike harbour, 20,000 acres in extent, reflected the city lights and those of the surrounding hills, where each house was an additional pinpoint of light. On nights such as this, visitors tend to agree that the harbour is the most beautiful in the country – and possibly in the world. Disembarkment would take place in the morning but in the meantime the fairyland scene was one to be savoured.

I stood at the ship's railings on the upper deck with Iris gazing down at the wondrous sight. By a stroke of Divine Providence, she, Frank and the children would be living in my parish, St Joseph's, so arrangements were made to complete the course of instruction.

The new immigrants were given their letters assigning them to different parts of the country, where they would be employed for two years in accordance with their contracts; after this time they could move to wherever they wished. Many of the Irish were assigned to the capital city and a few weeks later they assembled at St Joseph's church for Iris' reception into the Church. She received many mementoes and religious objects to mark the occasion.

Meanwhile, the *Captain Cook* was once more on its homeward journey, with Louis Gleeson as chaplain. For both Louis and me, this was a rich and rare pastoral experience, teeming with amazing grace and cherished memories. Iris' journey of faith will forever be the gem in the crown of my memories. Three children were born to her and Frank during their time in New Zealand: Jimmy – named after guess who; Jacinta, whom I baptised; and Bridget, who was known affectionately to me as 'the BBB' – Bridie the beautiful blonde!

The Carre family have now been back in Jersey for the past twenty years. Francis, the eldest, settled in New Zealand, and Jimmy settled in England. The three girls live close to their parents in Jersey. Iris and Frank made a surprise appearance at my Golden Jubilee celebrations in June. Iris put the glitter on the gold when she brought up the chalice in the offertory procession. Needless to say, we had lots to talk about and lots of memories to recreate – not least the Damascus Road experience on the Pacific Ocean.

10

Architect of an Earthquake

A quotation I would use about the creator of the earthquake comes from Shakespeare, not from Scripture. When Hamlet was examining Yorick's skull at Ophelia's graveside, he said, 'I knew him, Horatio, a fellow of infinite jest. His flashes of merriment were wont to set the table on a roar.' The subject of this chapter was first and foremost a man of God but also 'a fellow of infinite jest' whose flashes of merriment, culminating in the Greymouth Earthquake, set many a New Zealand table on a roar.

At the end of our first year in New Zealand, in the summer of 1952, Louis Gleeson and I went on holidays to the South Island. We crossed the Cook Strait, which separates the two islands, by ferry and then took the bus southwards to Dunedin, the Edinburgh of the south, thence to Invercargill and from there to the Bluff, the last town before Antarctica and the South Pole. In this long trek, never once did we have to stay in a hotel or bed and breakfast. Such was the deep-rooted tradition of clerical hospitality that every presbytery had an open door to visiting priests. Our trip was a never-to-be-forgotten experience of fraternity and newly created friendships.

It was the same on the return journey. Priest after priest welcomed us to his dwelling and drove us through breathtaking scenery in Southland and Central Otago. Then one evening we arrived in Christchurch, the Garden City, and made our way to the cathedral, where we introduced ourselves to the administrator, Gerry Kane. Gerry was a Meath man who welcomed us with open arms. After dinner he phoned every Irish priest in the city and invited them over to meet 'the two disciples from Tipperary'. Bishop Ted Joyce came along and we were deluged with invitations and offers of hospitality. That was the night I first met Jimmy Houlihan: it was a night to remember and the start of a cherished friendship.

Montalambert points out in *Monks of the West* that the Church has always sought certain qualities in its clergy – fraternity, benignity ... and hilarity. Jimmy had all these virtues in abundance, especially the medieval concept of *hilaritas*. This latter quality found its supreme expression in the famous 'Earthquake', which was conceived, devised and erupted in the Greymouth presbytery. It may not have been measured on the Richter scale but its tremors evoked peals of laughter and 'set every table on a roar' in his adopted country.

Shortly before he left on what turned out to be his last visit to his home in Gortnahoe, I spent a night with him in his Woolston presbytery in suburban Christchurch, and there he told me the story of the 'Earthquake' as only he could tell it. I am now telling it for the very first time, as all the *dramatis personae* have, like himself, gone to the Lord.

The fraternity outlined above, which was such a feature of clerical life in New Zealand in the middle of the last century, provides the backdrop for what follows. As Greymouth, capital of the Westland province, was the epicentre of this cataclysmic event, it behoves us to set the scene.

Westland province, where our story begins, could be regarded as a country within a country. It is a strip of rocky territory on the west coast of New Zealand's South Island. It is about 200 miles long and 40 miles wide and lies between the Southern Alps and the western shore. This province was scissored from the Canterbury province on the eastern side of the Alps in 1874, and the landscape on each side of the mountain range is as different as chalk and cheese. Where the Canterbury plains are flat and cultivated, the western terrain is hilly and rugged; where the east has a dreamy sameness, the west has profusion of spectacular scenery; where the east has major ports like Lyttleton, Timaru and Oamaru, the west has none except Greymouth. In fact the only thing the east and west have in common is that they are both part of the diocese of Christchurch. Even here the west is the poor relation. In the 1940s and 1950s the priests on the west coast were virtually cut off from their confrères in the east. Their only exit and entrance to the Canterbury

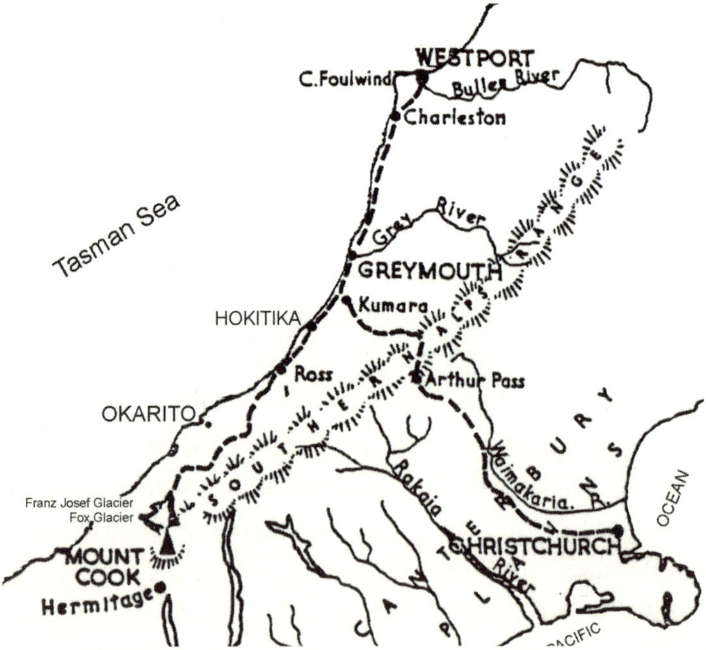

plains was the tortuous journey through Arthur's Pass and the Otira Gorge, by which they ascended seven miles to the summit.

Their relative isolation strengthened the bond of friendship, and the fraternal spirit of the priests on the west coast and the Greymouth presbytery was the focal point of this *esprit de corps*. Greymouth is the oldest parish in the province, founded in 1864 and dedicated to St Patrick – a tribute to the many Irish who came there in the gold-rush days. Twenty-five miles south of Greymouth is Hokitika, with its huge statue of a gold-digger, who could have been an Irishman. He is gazing at a pub. Regardless of whether or not the man was meant to be an Irishman, this monument to the unknown digger symbolises half a million or so gold-seeking adventurers, including many Irish, who rushed from field to field between Hokitika and Greymouth in quest of the pot of gold at the rainbow's foot and barely made their living expenses from all their toil.

The Greymouth presbytery was a haven for visiting priests. Monsignor James Long, a genial Limerick man, and his two assistants, Jimmy Houlihan, from Gortnahoe, and Arthur Gregory, a native son of the west coast, extended the hand of friendship and hospitality to all comers, including a certain monsignor from Christchurch who arrived on the doorstep one day and announced that he'd be staying for a week, and possibly two. The two curates saw an added bonus in the visit of the monsignor. If he would cover for them – and all that involved was saying a Mass in the church each morning – then they could set out on the trail leading to the glaciers and make fraternal visits to their confrères on the way. Some of these priests were in isolated outposts with sweet-sounding names – Maori names like Wataroa, Okarito and Mapourika – right down to the Franz Josef Glacier, named in honour of the Emperor of Austria. This glacier, rising in a snowfield of 6,000 acres (9,000 feet above sea level), is the overspill of the snow, compressed to a river of ice about half a mile wide, which slowly slips down a valley for nine miles before its edge thaws at the cliff only 690 feet above sea level, in the fern and palm forest at the foot of the range. Jimmy and Arthur planned to stay with their confrère in the Franz Josef township on the Waiho River and would walk with them through the fairy grass of the forest to the ice face, and then out onto the glacier, awed by the immensity of its shining vistas.

But alas, their dreams were shattered when the monsignor refused to cover for them. He told them that he was there on vacation and had no wish to be burdened with pastoral duties. Then he foolishly, as it later transpired, asked them if there was any risk of earth tremors – or, God forbid, worse – during his stay. There and then was conceived the plan to stage the famous earthquake.

The initial approach was psychological. The conversation at meals was skilfully directed to the topic of earthquakes and the apocalyptic forces that surge and boil beneath the crust of the Westland earth. Memories were recreated of the nearby Murchison earthquake, which obliterated homes and families and turned the entire area into a wasteland. When the monsignor's countenance took on a ghastly pallor, the plotters decided to move on to the second and more proximate stage. While their prospective victim was taking his constitutional stroll after lunch, they carried two sackloads of stones and bricks into the attic and strategically placed them near the trapdoor in the ceiling of the visitor's room.

That evening the conversation at dinner turned once more to earthquakes. The monsignor was notably silent during the discussion. Eventually he announced his intention of retiring early after he had had a bath. The conspirators decided that it was now or never. When the victim was soaking in the bath, Arthur took up his position in the attic and Jimmy got under the bed. The earthquake would erupt as soon as the monsignor turned off the light. When the countdown began, Jimmy noticed an open book on the bedside table with the visitor's spectacles resting on it. 'My God,' he said to himself, 'if he starts reading we'll be here all night!' So he solved the problem by hiding the spectacles.

When the hapless victim returned, he could be heard muttering, 'Now where did I leave those glasses?' Eventually he abandoned the search and proceeded to do some physical exercises, adding to Jimmy's discomfort. Finally he got into bed and turned out the light.

Then the mayhem started. Jimmy launched the earthquake by giving the bed a number of spasmodic jerks, which increased in intensity as the victim screamed. Stones and bricks began to fall from the ceiling as the panic-stricken monsignor fell out of the bed in an unholy heap. Jimmy turned the bed on top of him and then slipped out the door undetected, overturning a dressing table en route. When he finally extricated himself from the mess on the floor, he ran screeching out onto the corridor, where he was comforted by the pastor, Monsignor Long, who took him into his own quarters and gave him a strong jorum 'to steady himself'.

James Long played his part in the plot with calm aplomb, assuring his guest that he himself had sensed the approaching tremors and had had the good sense not to go to bed. As he comforted the monsignor, the sound of snoring could be heard emanating from the curates' rooms.

'Ah well,' the pastor sighed, 'they've been through this so often, they probably slept through it.' He then continued, on an ominous note, 'You know, this could be the harbinger of more catastrophic things to come.'

But the Christchurch prelate was having no more of it. He decided there and then to leave on the first train the following morning after he had celebrated Mass in the Mercy Convent next door. And there began the final act in the saga of Jimmy Houlihan's earthquake.

The superior of the convent was Mother Vincent Maguire from County Cavan, a towering figure in the story of the Mercy Order in New Zealand and destined shortly to become Mother General of her order. She too was an accessory to the conspiracy. She joined the monsignor at breakfast, accompanied by Sister Gertrude Joyce, sister of James.

'That was a terrible experience that you had surely, monsignor,' said Vincent, 'but sure we're used to these earthquakes, aren't we, Sister Gertrude?'

Gertrude nodded sagely.

Vincent then proceeded remorselessly to pile the agony on the traumatised monsignor: 'There could be a run of earthquakes now, but sure we take them as they come!'

The monsignor had had enough. Bidding a final farewell to Greymouth, he was on the train to Christchurch within the hour. Not until the train emerged from the six-mile

Otira tunnel and he saw the Canterbury plains stretching out before him did he heave a sigh of relief. He decided to continue his holiday, this time in the relative safety of Dunedin, where the news of the 'earthquake' had preceded him. He stayed in the cathedral presbytery, where he regaled Bishop James White and the clergy with his misadventure on the west coast.

Bishop White, a shrewd Kilkenny man with a twinkle in his eye, brought the monsignor across the road to the Dominican convent boarding school and got him to share his experience with the girls, who, no doubt, listened to him with rapt attention.

Years later, Jimmy Houlihan was on a visit to Dunedin and was taken to see Bishop White, now a chronic invalid in the Mater Hospital. On being introduced to the prelate, the old man gazed on him in awe and exclaimed, 'Ah! The earthquake priest!'

Shortly after Jimmy told me this story, he left on a visit to his homeland. He called to Ballinure to see my parents and told them of our friendship. One day, as his nephew drove him through the countryside where he grew up, Jimmy felt tremors of a different kind in the region of his heart. While he was telling a story, he died as he had lived, with a smile on his lips – a smile perhaps evoked by the prospect of meeting the monsignor way up yonder. He was just fifty-two years old. As luck would have it, his former pastor, Monsignor James Long, happened to be on holidays in Ireland at the time. Word was sent to him, so he came and celebrated the Funeral Mass of his erstwhile curate and later stood by the graveside as Jimmy was laid to rest in the brown earth of his native Tipperary, far from the towering mountains of Westland and the plains of Canterbury.

11

James Joyce – Epiphany – and Poppie

Margaret Joyce, who was 'Poppie' to her family, should have gone to New Zealand to enter the Sisters of Mercy in 1903 – and would have done so, had her mother not died that same year. After the funeral, Margaret's brother James besought her to remain on for a few years in a mother's role to the younger members of the family. She agreed, and during the six years before she joined the Sisters of Mercy she kept house for her father and her sisters and brothers: ten Joyce children – six girls and four boys – survived infancy. James was the oldest and Margaret was next in line. There was always a close, affectionate bond between them. Two years before Margaret became a nun, Joyce wrote to her from Trieste, asking if he could send his son Giorgio back to Dublin for a few weeks in the summer. The letter ends: 'Hoping this will find you as it leaves me at present, thank God, I am, dear sister, your most affectionate Brother.' Many accounts of Joyce, particularly in the light of his 'Epiphany', would lead us to believe that he turned against his family, his country and his Church, but they are not substantiated by family evidence. He returned to Ireland to see Poppie off to New Zealand in 1909 and he kept in regular touch with her until he died in 1941.

I first met Poppie in the summer of 1952. I was on a visit to the Mercy Convent in Papanui, a suburb of Christchurch in the South Island of New Zealand. In residence at the time was Sister Vincent Maguire, one of Jimmy Houlihan's accomplices in the Greymouth 'Earthquake' and now Superior General of the Mercy Order. It was she who suggested that I might like to meet Sister Gertrude (Poppie's name in religion). Poppie was now a member of the Papanui community, having spent almost forty years in Greymouth. Sister Enda, the local superior, had been shielding Poppie from the media and university students eager for information on Joyce's family background. But Poppie never gave interviews, so I was fortunate to be one of just two people – the other was Father Godfrey Ainsworth – with whom she shared her memories of growing up with Jim, as she called him.

Our first chat was over a cup of tea in the parlour in Papanui, when she freely recreated memories of growing up with her brother. 'We were always close,' she mused, 'and, being the eldest, were sometimes *in loco parentis.*' This was no doubt an allusion to the declining fortunes of the family: her mother's illness, her father's drinking and the instability produced by moving house on a regular basis.

'He had a lovely tenor voice,' she recalled, 'and we spent hours together at the piano. On one occasion, his name appeared on the same concert programme with John McCormack, though in much smaller print.'

A note of sadness crept into her voice as she recalled her brother's spiritual odyssey. 'Jim was the most religious of us all. As a matter of fact, he scared the rest of us with the intensity of his faith and some of his religious practices. He was a daily Mass-goer and he used spend at least one hour in Thanksgiving after Holy Communion. He was an avid reader, but never read a book during Lent – outside of his studies, that is. Besides,' she added, 'he was the elected president of Our Lady's Sodality at Belvedere College.'

She never read any of his works, so it is doubtful if she knew of his 'Epiphany' on Dollymount Strand, recounted in his *Portrait of the Artist as a Young Man,* when he made his final break – or so it seemed at the time – with religion, country and language, which he saw as the shackles preventing him from becoming a true artist:

> When the soul of a man is born, in this country, there are nets flung at it to hold it back from flight. You talk to me of nationality, language and religion. I shall try to fly by those nets.

To find art he must forsake religion, which he does as the story unfolds in the *Portrait*. With Parnell in mind, and also the 1916 leaders, he calls Ireland an 'old sow that eats her farrow'; and he turns his back on his country by going into exile. The triple renunciation is complete with *Finnegan's Wake* and, to a lesser extent, *Ulysses,* where he coins his own language.

His epiphany happens when he is walking on the strand near Dollymount. He sees a girl standing midstream, gazing out to sea. With her long, slender bare legs and her skirts kilted up about her waist, she looks like a strange and beautiful seabird. When she senses his gaze, she returns it without shame or provocation, gently stirring the water with her foot. We never discover who she is, nor does Stephen, the name Joyce gives himself in the *Portrait.* This experience is rich in myth and symbol. The girl rises from the sea like Venus, and she is like a bird because birds have special meaning for Stephen. Dedalus in legend was a bird-man. He made wings and flew. Joyce's break was complete, final and irrevocable. Or was it? We shall see.

Shortly before his epiphany, Margaret had told Joyce of her intention to enter the religious life. At the time of his fervour, he said to her, 'Why not do something really heroic and witness at the uttermost parts of the earth?'

When asked where this might be, his reply was, 'The Antipodes – and New Zealand, in particular. You can't get much further than there.'

'And that,' she added, 'is how I came to be here.'

There are many biographies of James Joyce, the most definitive being Richard Ellmann's magnum opus *Joyce.* In it, Ellmann said that her 'family life weighed so heavily on Margaret that it gave her a distaste for life in the world, and impelled her, a few years later, to become a nun.' Sister Gertrude was greatly distressed by this assertion, and her friend Godfrey Ainsworth was quick to bring this to the notice of Ellmann and to point out to him that genuine vocations to the religious life are not born of negative drives or drives of escape. And just as judgements have been passed on Sister Gertrude's vocation, so too has James Joyce's reputation in relation to family, country and church suffered through the years. To be fair to Richard Ellman, however, he omitted his erroneous assertion in the subsequent edition of his work.

My introduction to James Joyce came shortly after ordination, when I was given a copy of *A Portrait of the Artist*. For me, it is the most readable of all his works – a semi-autobiographical tale of his alter ego, Stephen Dedalus. It is a coming-of-age story like no other, the story of every child who has been bullied and terrorised, every adolescent who has ever burned with shame and sexual guilt. Who could ever forget his verbatim rendering of the hellfire sermon, preached in the school chapel, which convulsed him with horror, making him believe his commonplace sexual fantasies to be mortal sins? Or the dramatic episode at the family's Christmas dinner, where again, in a vividly remembered argument, he portrays the long-delayed hope of independence frustrated once more by the downfall of Charles Stewart Parnell.

In the home, the father is the embodiment of nationality, whereas the mother embodies religion. Her unquestioning acceptance is contrasted with her son's developing scepticism. The relationship between mother and son was heading for an impasse when he left for Paris in 1902, his departure a graphic expression of his revolt against nationality, family and religion.

Six months later he was summoned home to Ireland when Margaret wired him that their mother was dying. His ultimate rejection of religion was his refusal to kneel as the last rites were being administered. Margaret deeply resented this stance by James and his brother Stan and upbraided both of them for their lack of filial respect. This experience preyed so much on Joyce that he recalls it in the opening pages of *Ulysses.* When he returned later to see his sister off on her long voyage to the Southern Cross and went with her to the boat in Kingstown for the first stage of the journey to Liverpool, she told him as they parted that she was bringing with her the surplice in which he used to serve Mass and that she would pray unceasingly every day for his return to the faith. Joyce just smiled, assuring her that he would write to her regularly and that, if she ever wished to return home, he would gladly send her the fare. There are shades of this parting in the story of Eveline in *Dubliners.*

Sister Gertrude's last memory of her mother was the Franciscan habit in which she was laid out. It reminded her of the Third Order of St Francis; she was a member of this order and regularly attended services in Adam and Eve's church on the quays. The next time she saw the habit was at a retreat in Loreto, Papanui, given by the New Zealand Franciscan Father Godfrey Ainsworth. It was the beginning of a long and trusting friendship between Gertrude and the Franciscan. She permitted Godfrey to tape and edit their many conversations. These conversations exploded the myth of Joyce's self-imposed exile. 'Well, after all,' Gertrude said, 'he came home for my mother's passing, he came home again to see me off to New Zealand and he even came home to manage a cinema in Mary Street. On other occasions he called on his friends Pádraig Colum, Eugene Sheehy and William Fallon. He never really left Dublin,' she mused. 'He took Dublin with him.'

Father Ainsworth, who had privileged access to the letters Joyce sent to Margaret, told me that the number, frequency and regularity of the letters casts serious doubts on the finality of his break with his family. His concern for his sister Margaret is a case in point. Margaret entered the Mercy Order in Greymouth on the west coast of New Zealand's South Island with two other Irish girls in 1910. Her Profession took place in the Convent Chapel, Greymouth, on 13 July 1912. Greymouth was a port town and the gateway to the Fox and Franz Josef Glaciers, the Southern Alps and some of the most scenic lands in the world. She spent almost forty years of her religious life teaching music and ministering to the sick in Greymouth and nearby Runanga.

In 1929 there was an earthquake in Murchison, a hundred miles from Greymouth, which devastated the town and shattered the countryside for miles around. It made overseas news and Joyce, who was in Trieste at the time, sent an urgent cable to the convent to find out whether his sister was safe and offering to send her the fare, should she wish to come home. In 1949 Sister Gertrude moved to Christchurch, where she taught music to young boys in Loreto College, and here too I had the privilege of meeting and conversing with her.

With a question mark over his self-imposed exile, one cannot help wondering about Joyce's professed rejection of religion. Was it a case of the singer and not the song? Was his gripe against the institutional Church? Some of his friends took comfort in his regular attendance at Holy Week services in Paris. One of these friends, Moune Gilbert, recalls that he said to her once, 'You know, you must not imagine that the Catholic religion is the same in Ireland as it is in France. Here it is very *sympathique.*'

David Norris recalls in his article 'Who Killed James Joyce', which appeared in the *Irish Times* centenary issue, that Joyce's principal accusation against the Catholicism of his youth was that 'it sought to imprison the forces of spiritual animation in the rich metalwork of chalice and monstrance and it became so preoccupied with the intricacies of ritual and the miserable legalisms of canon law that it never noticed the withdrawal of the Holy Spirit from its weary ceremonials'. Joyce found this legalism of the Irish Catholic Church offensive.

All of Joyce's writings are permeated through and through by religion. Many of his most descriptive passages are woven in a religious loom. The opening words of the

Mass – *Introibo ad altare Dei* – introduce *Ulysses,* his *magnum opus.*

T. S. Eliot, in a conversation with Anthony Cronin, says that he has changed his mind on James Joyce and that he now regards him as a religious writer. Once, when discussing Thomas Merton and his writings with Sister Gertrude, Godfrey Ainsworth reminded her of the questions put to Merton by the Abbot of Gethsemane Abbey when the aspiring Trappist presented himself for admission to the monastery. He was asked what influenced him to convert firstly to Catholicism and secondly to monasticism. Unhesitatingly, Merton replied, 'The writings of James Joyce'.

Godfrey recalls how Gertrude's face lit up on receiving this piece of information. 'Just imagine,' she gasped, 'Jim doing this!' But Jim did even more. He did something for me too. Joyce had a blotting-paper memory. He never took notes during lectures. He didn't need to. His word-for-word rendition of the Retreat Lectures in Clongowes in *A Portrait of the Artist* bears witness to this.

Elsewhere in the *Portrait* he describes a university lecture given in Earlsfort Terrace. As most of the students are feverishly taking notes, he notices 'Another head, right before him in the first benches, was poised squarely above its bending fellows like the head of a priest appealing without humility to the tabernacle for the humble worshippers about him.'

These lines had a salutary effect on me. There's a prayer in the Mass which begins, 'In a spirit of humility and with a contrite heart ...' The priest now says it not leaning towards the tabernacle but inclined towards the humble worshippers in front of him. Ever since reading Joyce's words, I have tried to say that prayer with a little more sincerity and a little less hypocrisy and sometimes use the occasion to say a quiet prayer for James Joyce too.

Gertrude's parting request as I said farewell to her before returning to Ireland in 1957 was: 'Father, won't you pray for Jim?' She herself prayed incessantly for him – so much so that one is reminded of Ambrose's words to Monica when she came to him pleading for prayers for her son Augustine: 'Go thy way, woman, and God bless you, for it is impossible that the child of tears such as yours should perish.'

Until the time she died, Gertrude believed that the brother she loved, and to whom, under God, she owed her religious vocation, was reconciled before he died in Zurich on 13 January 1941. She kept in touch with Nora Barnacle and befriended her on many occasions. She was particularly interested in the couple's two children, Giorgio and Lucia.

Several months after Joyce died, a Jesuit priest, whom she knew only as Father Leonard, called to the Greymouth Convent and asked to see Sister Gertrude. The story he told her was to fill the rest of her life with serenity and joy.

On the night of James Joyce's death, Father Leonard was in Zurich. Actually, he told her, he was standing outside the door of the room in the hospital where her brother died, and he saw a priest come out of his room. He had come to New Zealand on a lecture tour but his purpose in coming to Greymouth was to see Sister Gertrude and convey this message to her: Joyce had a priest with him when he died. In retrospect, she concluded that Father Leonard himself must have been that priest. If not, why had he been standing outside Joyce's room in the early hours of the morning on that 13 January 1941?

Sister Mary Gertrude herself died on 1 March 1964. Sister Enda, who was her superior at the time of her death, was given the unenviable task of destroying all the letters she had received from Jim and Stan. It was Gertrude's express wish that everything – letters, mementoes and photographs – be destroyed. Fortunately, Godfrey Ainsworth's conversation tapes have survived and are in good condition; he has privately published transcripts of them.

12

Coming Home to Change

My years in New Zealand passed all too quickly. Louis was the first to receive the summons home. The cable from the Archbishop of Cashel to Peter McKeefry was short and cryptic: 'Please send Father Gleeson home.' Louis was straightaway on the phone to me, saying, 'Start packing your bags, Jim, you're next.' In the normal course of things, I should have been next in line when a vacancy occurred on the home mission, but providence stepped in when I was stricken with illness on the eve of Louis' departure. Shortly after I'd been to see the doctor, he called me to say that my X-ray revealed a collapse of the lower part of the left lung and I was to go to hospital immediately. Now a collapse of the lung in those days spelt just one thing – tuberculosis – and the dread TB meant isolation in a fever hospital. Wellington's Ewart Hospital might well have chosen as its maxim, 'Abandon hope, all ye who enter here'.

I checked into a Catholic hospital, where both Louis and I had been chaplains, to undergo the dreaded tests that might well send me to Ewart Hospital and Louis calling to say farewell did little to revive my drooping spirits. Now I was parting with my best friend and a friendship that had bound us together for over thirteen years: a friendship which had begun in the seminary and which had been sealed by the priesthood of Christ on 18 June 1950; a friendship which had deepened on the ocean liner that had taken us across the world to New Zealand and which had grown deeper and stronger in our years together under the Southern Cross. He too was visibly upset, because he had spent the last few days parting with friends whom he might never see again.

I can still see him standing at the end of my bed, more silent than usual. This I put down to pangs of parting, until he said finally, 'Do you know, I really envy you.'

'Ah, come off it!' I said, feeling like one of the gladiators of old addressing the Emperor with the words, *'Morituri te salutamus'* – 'We who are about to die salute you.'

'I'm deadly serious,' he went on, 'because the only time in this life that you can be absolutely sure that you are doing God's will is when you are sick.'

'How can you be so sure?' I asked.

'Because when you're ill, there's really nothing else that you can be doing, is there?'

Pearls of wisdom such as this were commonplace to Louis. Small wonder that so many people, not least myself, came to him for counselling.

The parting wasn't easy for either of us. Words were superfluous. The extra pressure in his handshake said it all. Next moment, he was gone.

My fears were unfounded. The tests, thank God, were negative. The ailment was diagnosed as atelectasis, a treatable condition caused by the collapse of a lobe of the lung. There was, however, one positive outcome. I was given an extra year in New Zealand to recuperate fully and to be fit to face the rigours of the Irish climate. At least that's how Peter McKeefry presented the case for an extension of my stay to my own archbishop.

I used this extra year of grace to pay a visit to the west

coast with two fellow priests. We spent our first night in the Greymouth presbytery, where Monsignor James Long welcomed us. The conversation over dinner was naturally dominated by the memories of Jimmy Houlihan and the 'earthquake'. James Long told us how privileged, yet saddened, he had been to officiate at Jimmy's obsequies in his native Gortnahoe. Then, turning to me with a mischievous grin, he asked, 'Would you feel safe if I put you into the earthquake room?' And so I slept in the very epicentre of Jimmy's earth-shaking escapade.

Travelling down the coast to the glaciers, we met a number of Irish priests in isolated outposts. We felt that we were offering them some slight compensation for Jimmy's aborted fraternal journey a few years previously. We passed through beautiful scenery to Wataroa, where we called on Father John Murphy, whose parish covers an area of 150 square miles. He visits his flock in remote areas four times a year by plane. From there, we travelled through snow-covered mountains, past beautiful lakes and across valleys covered with fern and native bush. We stopped at the Franz Joseph Glacier for tea, intending to return there on the morrow. The road from here to the Fox Glacier must be the twistiest in the world: there were no fewer than 365 turns in the space of fifteen miles. We arrived at the Fox around 8.30 pm and stayed in the hotel. Next morning we saw the wide, gleaming river of ice dropping nine thousand feet in nine miles. Then it was back to the twisty road to the Franz Joseph, where we stayed in a hotel owned by the O'Sullivan family, who had come in the gold-rush days. We visited St James' church, which was so designed that its east window behind the altar frames a glimpse of the glacier, giving an incomparable view of nature's gigantic magnificence:

Beauty is truth, truth beauty
That is all we know on earth
And all we need to know

If this is true, then beauty and truth were staring at us from the vista before us: beauty in the form of the glittering glacier spilling down from the snow-capped peaks of the southern Alps; truth in the realisation of how puny and insignificant man is in the presence of this masterpiece of the creator of the world – man, here today and gone tomorrow, while the mountains stand forever.

On 13 April 1957 – at 5 am, to be precise – I watched a beautiful sunrise on the Irish coast as the plane taking me home approached Shannon. As the green fields spread beneath me I reflected on how travel abroad had progressed in the short space of six years. Out to New Zealand by sea and home by air was a precursor of things to come. I came home to an Ireland that was on the threshold of change.

Change, of course, was always there, but for my generation change was an epochal thing that happened every thirty years or so. The new element was the speed of change. The transformation had begun with the economic development programme of Seán Lemass and T. K. Whitaker. The last period of dramatic change before the industrial process had been the War of Independence and the creation of De Valera's Ireland. Industrialists were now the dominant group; the weekly wage was higher than the seasonal income of farmers; new jobs were created by bringing in multinationals. Massive economic changes received the support of the State but not of the Church. The traditional concepts of faith and fatherland now became Church and State, helped on their way by the repercussions flowing from the collapse of Noel Browne's Mother and Child scheme in 1951. New battle lines were now being drawn between industry and agriculture; urban and rural; consumerism and idealism; secularism and religion. A process which took 2,000 years in western Europe occurred in Ireland in a much shorter time.

We had an awful lot thrown at us in the 1960s, particularly in the wake of the Second Vatican Council. On his return from a session of the Vatican Council, John Charles McQuaid declared, 'You have been worried by much talk of changes to come. Allow me to reassure you, no change will worry the tranquillity of your Christian lives.'

He came home unaware that the ground had moved under him. It was only when the liturgical changes became law – which happened in stages – that we realised we were travelling through uncharted territory. For some, the transition was easy; for others, it was a painful experience. These changes shattered the tranquillity of many lives, particularly those of the generation above us, who were sadly and pitiably destabilised.

Nora Hickey, our housekeeper in the Thurles presbytery, was one of those who did not take kindly to the changes in the Church. 'That auld Pope John,' she muttered. 'He's after ruining the religion!' Nora was one of a group who had deserved well of the Church, had worked and worshipped in conditions of great hardship and felt undermined in the evening of their days. I have seen her grieving for some of the things she'd been asked to give up, such as the Mass she loved and that her parents and grandparents loved. She could not accept Eucharistic ministers and Communion in the hand and she was appalled by the disappearance of the altar-rails – one of the features of the reordering of churches in the 1970s. But it was the changed feeling of the Mass that really upset her, and there was no mechanism to allow Nora to grieve for what she was losing. As a result, she vented her feelings on us, her partners in grief. 'Look at what ye've done to the Mass!' she would say. 'Sure now we can't say a prayer or do a round of the beads with all that blathering that goes on at the altar. The Mass is all we have left and ye're after making a feck of that too!'

Pity the poor preacher too. He was left standing by the communications revolution. The ambo replaced the pulpit, sermons became sermonettes and the homily became a sort of spiritual *hors d'oeuvre* before Holy Communion. Add to that the massive boredom in the pews, the people – especially the young – voting first with their concentration and then with their feet. The preacher had to face the sometimes unpalatable fact that education and changing attitudes to authority figures were making people more critical. They would no longer accept the drivel that was sometimes doled out to them, nor would they tolerate the use of the pulpit as a launching pad for the bees that buzz in preachers' bonnets. He had to deal with a television-conditioned congregation which could no longer listen without looking, and he could no longer assume that they either wanted to listen or were able to do so. Attentive faces were no guarantee of attentive minds. We had passed from a word culture to a picture culture without realising it.

Father Gerard Arbuckle, the New Zealand Marist, in his work *Grieving for Change* talks about the phenomenon of grieving, pointing out that grief is a very important part of human existence. In this country, the old custom of keening at wakes was the ritualising of the basic need of every human heart, in a time of bereavement, to grieve. Part of the joylessness and low morale in the priesthood, not just in the wake of the Second Vatican Council but more especially in the Church today, is that we have all been through a period of great grief; we didn't realise that it was grief and there was no mechanism in the Church – nor is there now – telling us how to cope with it. I have in mind particularly what is now categorised as the scandals in the Church. These have diminished all of us so much that many priests in urban areas have given up pastoral visitation in fear of what might be said to them on the doorstep. One man was told, 'I'm sorry, Father, there are no children here.'

Another source of concern has to be the shepherds in the mist – the priests who have left the ministry. What has been our attitude to them? To be judgemental? To cut them off? How do we communicate with them?

Or again, there is the cold, clinical manner in which priests are appointed to parishes – and, especially, removed from them – without even the elementary courtesy of advance consultation. For many priests to be moved in this manner, at the stroke of a bishop's pen, is a form of bereavement and a source of deep-rooted grief. Peter McKeefry, with a diocese much larger than Ireland and straddling the two islands of New Zealand, never appointed a priest to a parish, or removed him, without first discussing the move with the man concerned. That is what made him the focal point and inspiration of that fraternity which was the hallmark of his priests.

Amongst the more positive aspects of change in the aftermath of the Second Vatican Council were the greater openness in the Church, especially to ecumenism; the vernacular in the Mass; the relaxation of the Eucharistic fast; the new rite of Penance; the Saturday-evening Mass; and the new emphasis on preparing children for the sacraments. On the other side of the coin, some saw the Vigil Mass as a threat to the Sabbath and there were reservations about the new religious programme for children. The loss or diminution of the sense of sin, coupled with the dual stance of some of the clergy in the contraception issue in the 1960s, led to a drop in Confessions. The fall in vocations became a cause for concern and has become a crisis situation now. It was, in the words of Dickens, the best of times and the worst of times.

Priests were subjected to a barrage of questions from a confused laity. Why is it no longer a sin to go into a Protestant church? What about all the ones ye sent to hell for eating meat on Friday? In retrospect, I can't see how the good and merciful Lord could be bothered with our legalism and stupid sentences. Speaking for myself, my credo became a simple one: God was the only security left in the midst of change, and faith, from being an assent to certain revealed doctrines, became a total surrendering of oneself into God's hands. We could see that the old ways were dying, that a new vision of the Church as the people of God was emerging and that God was to be found amongst his people, particularly the homeless, the poor and the marginalised. Something new was happening. The Church was saying openly, the Divine penetrates the human, the Incarnation transforms the created universe and we must be part of that transformation.

Two men, who were a part of that transformation and who touched my life in a very special way because in them I was given a glimpse of the Divine penetrating the human, are the subjects of the valedictories that follow.

13

Louis and James – Men of God

'I glorified thee on earth, having accomplished the work which thou gavest me to do' (John 17:4). Only one person could ever dare to say these words. To one alone could they ever apply. That one is Jesus Christ, our Lord. But there are a few who, their earthly journey over, more nearly approximate to the ideal sketched in these words than do most of us. Louis Gleeson and James Meehan were two of these. There was a singular completeness about the life's work of each of them. God had given them a great work to do, and they had done it with humility, dedication and distinction. They worked right up to the day and the hour when the Lord called them. They literally died with their boots on. All three of us entered the seminary on the same day; we were ordained together on the same day.

Louis Gleeson (1925–77) needs no introduction to anyone who has been reading this book thus far, so biographical data are superfluous. I could write about Louis as a priest, but even here words seem totally inadequate. I have already referred to Louis Gleeson as counsellor: how many time have I gone to him with my personal problems, received a sympathetic ear – as did many other people – and come away refreshed, consoled and comforted. I could also write of Louis as a preacher whose sermons were carefully prepared and delivered with sincerity and conviction, and it is significant that on his last day on earth he preached at two Masses in Templemore on the first Sunday of Advent. His theme was the secularisation of Christmas. He even sang a verse of 'Jingle Bells' to illustrate the emptiness of the world's celebration of the Saviour's birth.

These are subjects that I could have chosen, but I want to probe deeper, because what use is a man as a priest, a counsellor, a visitor or a preacher unless he is first and foremost a man of God. His priesthood will be empty and hollow. His preaching will be mere words, even though he may speak them eloquently. His counselling may be merely good advice. His visiting will be merely talking about the weather or hurling matches, unless he is first and last a man of God.

The first time the Scriptures mention those three words – 'man of God' – is in a homely little story that is tucked away in the fourth chapter of the second book of Kings. It is about the prophet Elisha, who was, like Louis, a great one for keeping in touch with his flock: almost every reference to him finds him visiting someone. In this little story, we are told that, when he was out visiting, he used to call into a house on the way and this woman would always give him a meal. The significant thing is that Elisha's character so impressed the woman after each visit that she could only describe him to her husband in these words: 'A holy man of God who is continually passing our way.' Had she been transported in time to Wellington, Drangan or Templemore, she might well have described Louis in similar terms.

'A holy man of God who is continually passing our way.' Notice that it was the sheer holiness of Elisha that impressed the Shunemite woman. I got so obsessed with the idea of the 'man of God' that I began to search the Scripture again. The only definition of it that I could find was in the sixth chapter of Paul's first letter to one of his first priests, Timothy, where I saw the phrase simply leaping off the page: 'But you, oh man of God!' In the next phrase Paul tells Timothy to shun certain things and to pursue other things; in the things to be shunned and pursued will be found the inner meaning of being 'a man of God'. Here is what Paul said, set in its full context (1 Timothy 6:6–12):

> There is a great gain in godliness with contentment; for we brought nothing into the world, and we cannot take anything out of the world; but if we have food and clothing, with these we shall be content. But those who desire to be rich fall into a temptation, into a snare, into many senseless and hurtful desires, that plunge men into ruin and destruction. For the love of money is the root of all evils; it is through this craving that some have wandered away from the faith and pierced their hearts with many pangs. But as for you, man of God, shun all this, aim at righteousness, godliness, faith, love, steadfastness, gentleness. Fight the good fight of the faith; take hold of the eternal life to which you were called when you made the good confession in the presence of many witnesses.

'But you, oh man of God.' Paul could have addressed these words to Louis Gleeson with the same sincerity and truthfulness as when he first said them to Timothy nearly 2,000 years ago.

Louis' two homilies on that first Sunday of Advent were firmly rooted in the Gospel of the day and its admonition to be prepared 'as you know not the day nor the hour'. The day, 27 November 1977, had arrived and the hour was fast approaching, but there was still time to bring Holy Communion to a sick mother, play two sets of tennis and make a phone call to his home in Clogher at 1.30 pm. He hung up the phone and, still sitting in his chair, passed quietly into the Eternal Vision.

Where does one even begin to tell the story of that other man of God that was James Meehan? The bare facts can be quickly set out. He was born in 1922 and died in 1992. Educated at Clonmore National School and Templemore Christian Brothers School in County Tipperary, he started for the priesthood with Louis Gleeson and myself in St Patrick's College, Thurles, in 1942, went on with us to Maynooth in 1943 and was ordained in the national seminary in 1950. Three curacies followed: the first on the outskirts of Glasgow, followed by six years in South Tipperary in the village of New Inn, and thence to Thurles for all of twenty-two years. In 1982 he returned to New Inn as parish priest, and in 1991, a year before his death, he became a born-again curate! He coined this title himself as an apologia for his decision to step down from the office of parish priest.

As you can see, it is a very simple story. Or is it? During James' lifetime a terrace of new houses was named after him; a few weeks after his death a public park was dedicated to his memory; less than a year after his death his biography was written and a wayside shrine appeared in south Tipperary carrying the simple message: 'In memory of Father James Meehan – Priest of the People; Priest of the Poor.' I spent eight years with him in the seminary and another seventeen years in Thurles presbytery. Twenty-five years under the same roof was longer than he had spent with any member of his immediate family, so I probably knew him as well as many and possibly better than most. But then, did anyone really know him?

The list of paradoxes and enigmas in his life, linked by a peculiar blend of naivety and cuteness, is seemingly endless. Revered by the people and devious to his peers; venerated by the homeless and downtrodden and resented by many of the settled communities, who objected to his refugees from the roads; tea with the queen in Buckingham Palace and tea from a tin mug with the travelling people on a country roadside; singing 'God Save the Queen' among the Rangers supporters at Ibrox one Saturday and singing 'The Soldier's Song' among the Celtic supporters at Parkhead the next; preaching to the British Legion on Poppy Day and laying a wreath with the Old IRA on Easter Monday; man of God to his friends and social activist to his critics – the perennial confusion between the perspiration of activity and the inspiration of God. These apparent contradictions, and many others, all find their rationale in a man who preached the Gospel to the poor on Sunday and revealed Christ to the people on Monday; a man who was all things to all men; one who was, in truth, a man for all seasons.

A stained-glass life of James Meehan would have to include the following inspirational tableaux: the shabby priest riding his bicycle in a battered hat, baggy pants and a dead man's overcoat; literally taking the shirt off his back and giving it to a traveller to wear at his mother's funeral; the small car towing a mobile home to a homeless family. The centrepiece would have to be the trailer, with its motley collection of mattresses, beds, wardrobes, prams, fuel and, on more than one occasion, goats – all destined for the needy. These little vignettes do him scant justice, for if one man in his life plays many parts, then James Meehan, champion of the poor, fool for Christ, lovable rogue, yet always the man of God, has more than exceeded his quota.

Perhaps an explanation is called for as to how James

came to be singing 'God Save the Queen' in Ibrox and later dining with the said queen in Buckingham Palace. The Rangers connection began in 1953, when Louis Gleeson was returning to New Zealand after a brief visit home. He stayed with James near Glasgow prior to his departure. Now it happened that on the day of Louis' arrival the Coronation Cup match between the Scottish champions, Glasgow Celtic, and the English champions, Arsenal, was taking place at Hampden Park. There was a stampede for tickets. James failed to get them in any of the usual Catholic outlets. So what did he do? He stuffed Louis and himself into a taxi and drove to Ibrox, the home of Rangers and the headquarters of Scottish bigotry, and asked to meet the general manager. The shock of seeing two priests that close nearly killed the manager. 'This here priest,' said James, 'is off to New Zealand. He'll be sick and sore and alone for five weeks on a ship. Could you ever, at all, in your power and goodness get a ticket for him?' The general manager, still in a state of shock, gave him two!

This was not to be James' only encounter with Rangers. In the course of house visitation, he came across a genial Protestant, Tommy Thomson, who invited him into his home. It was the beginning of a beautiful friendship. James' host turned out to be the chairman of the Rangers supporters club, and he too would not see his guest short of tickets for the remainder of his stay in Scotland. And that explains how James, a Catholic priest, found himself belting out 'God Save the Queen' among some of the most partisan and sectarian supporters in British football. When the call to return to Ireland came in 1954, the people gathered in St Columba's Hall to bid him a last farewell. The highlight of the evening was a presentation made to him by the Glasgow Rangers Supporters Club. This was unprecedented in the history of the Church in Scotland. It had never happened before; it has not happened since.

James Meehan is the only priest of the archdiocese – and perhaps of any other Irish diocese, for that matter – to have been received by the queen in Buckingham Palace. It all happened through Katie the war widow. Katie had been left destitute on the death of her husband, who had been a veteran of the First World War. When he died, his pension was cut off and Katie came to James with her hardship story. He immediately contacted the headquarters of the British Legion and in due course was invited to appear at a tribunal in Dublin which was specially set up to deal with Katie's plight.

From the outset, the British Legion assumed that James had been in active service and, needless to say, he neither said nor did anything to disillusion them. So impressed were they by his interest in their activities and the sincerity of his plea for the widow, that they appointed James as their official representative in the Thurles area to look after the interests of all the war widows. Next came an invitation to preach at the Remembrance Day ceremonies in St Patrick's cathedral. Mounting the pulpit that had been graced by the great Dean Jonathan Swift and displaying his red poppy, he delivered his homily on the glorious dead in a cathedral festooned with banners commemorating battles long ago. He then looked on bemused as bemedallioned survivors of the First World War with heaving chests belted out the Protestant hymns.

Then, one morning as we were having breakfast in the

presbytery, a large square envelope arrived. There it was in gold lettering: Her Gracious Majesty requested the presence of Father James Meehan at a Royal Command Garden Party to be held in the grounds of Buckingham Palace. The invitation was accompanied by a document setting out the rules of etiquette for the occasion. As he read through it, he passed the wry comment, 'God, lads, she must have been told about the trailer. She wants me to arrive at the palace by taxi!'

Accustomed as he was to wearing dead men's clothes, he now treated himself to the rare luxury of a new suit and set off to meet the queen. The taxi driver was so chuffed at the honour of bringing a passenger to meet royalty that he insisted on being photographed with James at the palace gates. He was an instant hit with the specially invited guests, who were sounding him out on which branch of active service he had been engaged in – queries which he deftly kicked to touch by reminding his interrogators that 'because of the troubled situation at home, careless talk could cost lives'! He was duly presented to the queen and Prince Philip, who thanked him for his services on behalf of the war widows.

Back in Ireland, when we asked him for his impressions of the queen, he described her as 'a grand little shtump of a woman, very aisy to talk to'. All of which goes to show that, as the occasion demanded, he could be all things to all men, as well as being a bit of a rogue into the bargain!

The chances of a parish priest ever becoming a saint – a canonised one, that is – are practically nil. At least that's what we were told by Tom Cleary, our spiritual director in Maynooth. He told us that John Vianney, the Curé of Ars, was the only one who made the grade. He set the standard for the rest of us. On one occasion, a young priest came to the saintly Curé seeking advice. His parish priest, ailing and gone in years, had announced his intention of retiring. The young man tried to prevail on him to stay on, but without success. Then he asked if he might seek the advice of the Curé of Ars, and the old man agreed. The Curé listened to the story and advised that his colleague should stay on. *'Sa presence serait un bien infini,'* he said – 'His presence will be of infinite benefit.'

The Curé put his finger on the basic element of priestly holiness: the priest as presence. Presence is the first influence in our lives and it precedes doing. *Agere sequitur esse,* we were taught in the seminary – 'to act follows to be'. The primary verb is 'to be'. The pastoral priest inspires by his presence. He will be remembered for what he is rather than for what he says or does. The priest is called to be a sign and sacrament of God's presence in the world. People want the presence of the holy, and the presence that attracts people and kindles their hope is the presence of a man who is free – free from idolatry, the first sin. Crom Cruach and his twelve subgods are very much with us today: the false gods of the world – money, power and pleasure – seek to capture the human heart. The priest who is free from these is a sure sign that the world is not God-forsaken; he is a sign and a sacrament of God earthed among us.

Frances Gleeson, a columnist with *The Tipperary Star* in a published tribute to James, wrote, 'If I ever saw Christ in any human being, I saw him in Father Meehan. What higher tribute can I pay him?' She recognised the holiness of presence and in James Meehan she found the presence of the holy. Unfortunately, in the times in which we live people are defined by their jobs and assessed by their status. In this way the person is devalued and presence has no power. This thought is reflected in a homily given by James a few months before he died: 'We place too much emphasis on jobs, positions, education and status. It is not what we do that matters with God. It is the kind of people we are. It is what I am that is of most importance.'

And what was he? A priest present in faith and freedom and representing God by his presence. It was this Christlike presence which empowered and animated his apostolate to the poor, the homeless and the travelling people, because in each one of them he saw the face of Christ. This is borne out by the following prayer, which he said daily: 'Lord, let me never forget that anyone blind or deaf, anyone crippled or lame, anyone cold or hungry, anyone needing a home and shelter is not just anyone, but is really you in disguise.'

When James Meehan took up the cause of the travelling people in 1954, he was very much on his own. The national organisations now speaking on behalf of travellers were not even conceived; there was no protection for them at government level, or indeed at any level. The government and local authorities saw them as a subculture of poverty, as drop-outs from the settled community. There was little or no support for them from the Church, which had not yet awoken to its responsibility of providing special pastoral care for the travelling community – apart, that is, from the basic preparation of travellers' children for Communion and Confirmation. Travellers with twice the mortality rate of the settled community died and were buried in make-shift coffins without even the consolation of a Mass to mark their obsequies. James was soon to find out that many priests shared with the settled community the same prejudices and hostility to the travellers.

What endeared James Meehan to the travelling community and made him so relevant to them was not so much the material succour he provided them in the form of food, clothing and shelter as the fact that he respected their dignity, recognised their culture and treated them as equals. He called them by their names and sat with them on the roadside and in their caravans and mobile homes. He coaxed, cajoled and plagued local authorities and public representatives to provide them with decent housing, and when he succeeded he came with his trailer laden with furniture, bedding, prams and sewing machines – anything that was required to set them up in decent living conditions. Inevitably, his efforts incurred the wrath and hostility of the respectable colony of the settled, who thwarted him at every turn, refusing to accept his refugees from the roads.

Time and again he was taken for a ride by some of the travellers. They would disappear with the mobile home he had purchased for them and repayments would cease. At one stage he was in debt to the tune of £12,000, until some generous benefactors came to his rescue.

When the Lord sent the twelve disciples out to evangelise and told them to be as wise as serpents and as simple as doves (Matthew 10:16), he seemed to be looking for irreconcilable attributes in his first priests. Perhaps, as in the case of Jeremiah, he had James Meehan in his mind's eye: 'Before I formed you in the womb I knew you, and before you were born I consecrated you' (Jeremiah 1:4). James had no problem with reconciling the seemingly irreconcilable.

Humility and kindness he had in abundance, but there were times when he could be as cunning, cute and devious as any latter-day politician. There are stories galore to illustrate this devious side of his personality. Here is a classic example that is true in every detail. Only the names have been changed.

Sam was not Gospel-greedy; he was rarely to be seen at Mass. Sal, his wife, was, however, a regular visitor to the presbytery, on the quest for handouts. One day James accosted Sam and suggested to him that he might make that little extra effort and pay an occasional visit to the cathedral. Sam assured him that all that was keeping him from his duties was the lack of proper footwear. 'If I had a dacent pair of boots, Father,' he declared, 'I'd be the first man into the house of God on Sunday.'

Shortly afterwards, James called to a house in which there had been a recent bereavement and asked the widow if her husband had left any presentable footwear, whereupon the good lady parted with a pair of boots which she assured him had only been worn three or four times. James returned to his car, took off his shoes and put on the dead man's boots before driving up to the terraced houses where Sam and Sal lived.

Entering the house, he again pleaded with Sam to come to Mass the following Sunday. 'Now, Father,' said Sam, eyeing the priest's newly shod feet, 'if I had a dacent pair of boots to put on my feet, like what you're wearing yourself, Father, saving your presence, I'd be down there like a flash every Sunday. I would as true as God!'

James sat down and began to unlace the boots.

'All right,' he sighed, resignedly. 'If they bring you to

Mass, I'll give you what I have on me.'

There was a shocked reaction from Sam and Sal. 'Ah, Father,' said Sal, 'sure we couldn't take the boots off your sacred feet. Sure we'd never have a day's luck if we did that to you!'

'If they take Sam to Mass, they'll be well worth it,' James repeated, handing over the boots.

In the torrent of gratitude that followed this heroic gesture, Sam assured him that he'd be 'the first man to cross the threshold of the house of God on Sunday morning.' And Sal promised, 'I won't come begging to ye again for three months, as God is me judge!'

James was deluged with blessings as he left the house and made his way towards a group of women who were chatting on the pavement nearby. Having bid them the time of day and engaged in a few pleasantries, and having observed a few furtive glances at his feet he continued on, bootless, to his car, feeling sure that they had got the message. Getting into his car, he put on his shoes and drove away.

The story soon spread – and lost nothing in the telling – that 'Poor Father Meehan was walking the streets in his socks after Sam and Sal had taken the boots off him!' James had the smug satisfaction of knowing that Sam was now happy with his new boots; that he'd be at Mass from now on; that the presbytery would be spared the supplications of Sal for at least three months; and, not least, that the entire operation had not cost him one penny!

As in the case of Louis Gleeson, James Meehan's last day on earth, 24 June 1992, was a flurry of activity: he cycled to Mass, made a number of pastoral calls and finally called to a priest, Father Noel O'Connor, who was about to return to the missions, with a generous donation. James was unable to get out of the car, so the young priest gently eased him into the passenger seat, removed his collar and shoes and administered the last rites. He then rushed him to Our Lady's Hospital, Cashel. But time was already running out for James; hours were now reduced to minutes. The final act of self-giving took place when he died in the hospital elevator. The lift was ascending at the time: he was being taken up.

No words seem to have been spoken by James as he died in the hospital elevator. What need had he of exit lines when his crowded life was full of them. One of them is worth recalling yet again – his words as he unloaded his trailer by a wayside caravan: 'I don't want to go up to auld Peter with empty hands.'

It was an exit line and a curtain call rolled into one.

14

Archbishop Croke, Parnell and Nora Hickey

You may well ask who is Nora Hickey? And what is she doing in the august company of the archbishop of Cashel and Parnell, the uncrowned king of Ireland? Wouldn't Croke, Parnell and Catherine O'Shea have been a more reasonable, if not more acceptable, trio? This is a fascinating story now being revealed for the first time, but first a word on Nora.

She was our housekeeper in the Thurles presbytery and a character cast in a different mould to John B. Keane's *Moll*, but a character nevertheless. Her parents died when she was young and her aunt in Thurles reared her. Her eldest brother, a brigadier in the British army, secured her first posting for her as maid-cum-receptionist in the castle of one of the royal dukes. Shortly after her arrival, there was a banquet to which the royalty and the surrounding nobility were invited. Nora's task was to answer the doorbell, curtsey to her 'betters' and escort them to the drawing-room. In the afternoon, the duchess, concerned that some of the ingredients for the *hors d'ouvres* had not arrived, sent for Nora and asked her if the partridges had come.

'No, ma'am,' said Nora, with a curtsey.

'That's strange,' said the duchess. 'They were to be here at 4 o'clock.'

'Well, if they came, missus,' said Nora, 'I didn't let them in.'

Anyway, our story begins in the presbytery one evening, when Nora was serving us more humble fare than partridges. The conversation was about Charles Kickham. An anniversary lecture on the Fenian patriot was being delivered that evening in the Hotel Munster next door, and I suggested to my colleagues that we should be represented at this talk, when Nora, who was gathering the dishes, interjected, 'Wasn't he the auld lad that Dr Croke booted out of the palace?'

'What auld lad?' I asked.

'That auld lad ye're talking about. Didn't Dr Croke kick his bust out of the palace?'

'No, Nora,' I replied. 'You're confusing Charles Kickham with another Charles – Charles Stewart Parnell.'

'Oh, I know a lot about Kickham,' said Nora, scoring a palpable hit. 'Didn't yere crowd lock the doors of the cathedral on him and wouldn't let in his coffin, just because he was a Fenian.'

'Oh, touché, touché, Nora,' I sighed, explaining to Nora that one of my predecessors, a Father Cantwell, would not receive Kickham's remains in the cathedral, not even for one night as they were *en route* for their final place in Mullinahone. I was quick to point out, however, that Archbishop Croke was on the continent at the time, and on his return he stated publicly in the cathedral that, had he been there, he would have honoured Kickham and that we were making some small amends by going to the Kickham lecture that evening.

Mention of Dr Croke brought Nora back to the bust, so I gave her a short précis of its history. The bond of friendship between Croke and Parnell was so strong that the uncrowned king, as he was called at the time, was a guest in the palace on many occasions, particularly at election time, when the archbishop actively campaigned for him. Parnell had three busts of himself commissioned: one for Catherine O'Shea, one for his friend Dr Croke and one for Avondale.

The bust had an honoured place in the palace until the scandal of Parnell's illicit relationship with Catherine O'Shea became public. Such was Croke's outrage and anger that he literally booted the bust out the front door of the palace. This is a fact verified and recorded in the biographies of Croke and Parnell.

'And that, Nora,' I concluded, 'is the story of the bust of Parnell.'

'Where is it now?' she asked, somewhat tentatively.

'Lost forever, I'm afraid, beneath layers of garbage in the Thurles dump.'

'It isn't,' she replied, 'because I have it.'

Before I could recover from my amazement, she continued, 'Do you want it? Because if you do, you can have it.'

'Is this on the level?' I gasped.

'It is, and if you don't believe me, come up to my house and see it for yourself. And if you want it,' she repeated, 'you can take it away with you.'

She then went on to tell us how it had come into her possession. Mrs Fogarty, her aunt, who, as we have seen, was *in loco parentis* for Nora as she grew up, was on very friendly terms with Croke's housekeeper, who, without the archbishop's knowledge, had rescued the bust from oblivion and entrusted it to Mrs Fogarty for safe keeping. When the entire *dramatis personae* had died, Nora became the possessor and sole owner of the bust.

I went home with Nora that evening, and I'm afraid

that, in the excitement of the occasion, I missed the Kickham lecture. But who could blame me, because there in Nora's kitchen was the long-lost bust of Parnell. It was him all right – easily identifiable, despite the many layers of paint he had received every time the kitchen was painted. It went through all the colours of the prism from sky-blue to deep red, but now thankfully it had reverted to its original white.

The final act in the drama took place on the following Friday evening, when Archbishop Thomas Morris, Croke's successor, came to tea in the presbytery, as was his weekly custom. I had strategically placed the bust on a sideboard directly facing the archbishop. More than once, he lost the thread of the conversation as his eyes became riveted on the figure facing him.

'Tell me,' he said at length, 'is that the one I think it is?'

'And who might that be?' I countered.

'It must surely be Parnell!'

'It is surely,' I replied.

'Tell me again, would it be, by any chance, the same as the one which my illustrious predecessor unceremoniously kicked out of my house?'

'One and the same!' I confirmed, and I then went on to tell him the story thus far.

'Oh my God,' he exclaimed, 'will you give it to me and I'll restore it to where it properly belongs?'

'Willingly,' I said, adding mischievously, 'it cost me a bottle of brandy.'

'I'll give you a case of brandy for it,' he rashly promised, which promise he mercifully soon forgot.

He took the bust in his arms and I accompanied him to his residence and photographed him as he carried it across the threshold. He placed it on a hallstand directly facing a life-size oil painting of Croke, and there it rests to this day. Whenever I see it, I try to read the expression on Croke's lips. He seems to be saying, 'You're back again, ye divil ye!'

Yes, the king was well and truly back in the palace!

The heroine of this story is, of course, the lovely big-hearted Nora Hickey, now gone to join Croke and Parnell in what is hopefully a blessed Trinity. She provided the inspiration for the first novel of one of Ireland's most successful and best-selling young writers, Mark O'Sullivan, who had been her *protégé* since he was a child. He thoughtfully called his book *Melody for Nora*. For those of us who are left with cherished memories of Nora, the melody will forever linger on.

15

THE POPE AND THE BISHOP'S DAUGHTER

I am indebted to my friend the late Colonel S. J. Watson, biographer of Charles Bianconi, King of the Irish Roads, for the following story. An old Etonian, Sydney put so much scholarly research into the romance as to make the incredible sound credible. The chapter heading is the stuff that tabloids are made of, but when you consider that the girl in the dalliance was the daughter of a Protestant bishop in an Ulster diocese and that the Pope of Rome, to whom she gave her heart and was more than willing to give her hand in marriage, was none other than the recently beatified Pio Nono – yes, he of the First Vatican Council and the infamous *Syllabus of Errors* – you can feel the bounds of credibility being stretched.

Now, mind you, he was not yet Pope when he first met Letitia Foster, daughter of the Right Reverend William Foster, Bishop of Kilmore, but he was certainly earmarked for the exalted position. He was Count Giovanni Maria Mastai-Ferretti, an officer in the Guardia Nobile, the Pope's bodyguard.

Bishop Foster (1744–97) was married to Catherine Letitia Leslie of Ballybay, County Monaghan, predecessor of Sir Shane Leslie, of whom more anon. There were seven children of this union – two sons and five daughters, of whom Letitia was the youngest. The tale which I will now unfold was first recorded by Augustus Hare in *The Story of My Life*, published in six volumes between 1896 and 1900, where he states that it was told to him by Dr Hawtrey. The Reverend Edward Craven Hawtrey was headmaster of Eton between 1834 and 1852 and subsequently provost. He was the last person to be buried in Eton College chapel. His mother was Elizabeth Foster, a close relation of the bishop.

The story, as told by Hawtrey, begins with Harriet, another daughter of Bishop Foster's, who married, against her parents' will, an Italian Casanova, a Count Jerome Fare de Salis. This count took her to a hired villa at Belloguardo near Florence, where, according to Hawtrey, he was exceedingly unkind to her, submitting her to an unremitting sequence of pregnancies from which she was mercifully released by his death. She returned to her parents in Ireland on the verge of a nervous breakdown. The harrowing memory of her ordeal at Belloguardo so haunted her that her doctor urged her to return to Florence now that her husband would no longer be there in order to exorcise it from her memory. She went back to Italy, accompanied by her younger sister, and there they met Count Mastai-Ferretti, the future pontiff, and he and Letitia Foster promptly fell in love.

Harriet, knowing that their parents would measure a foreign marriage by her own dreadful life with the Count de Salis, wrote to them, assuring them that in Count Mastai they must imagine the exact opposite of Count de Salis. Harriet informed them that Count Mastai was honourable, chivalrous, noble, generous – in fact, that had she to seek through the whole world for the person to whom she could commit her sister's happiness with the greatest confidence, she would choose Count Mastai.

The wedding day was fixed, the wedding dress was

made and the wedding feast was prepared. When the day came all the friends of Madame de Salis collected in the church of San Luigi de Francesci, where the marriage was to take place. According to the then custom in Rome, Miss Foster, accompanied by Madame de Salis, came first to the altar and waited for the bridegroom. He never came. Letitia was literally left standing at the altar.

The Hawtrey account alleges that Miss Foster's fiancé was inveigled away from her because he had been summoned on a Jesuit mission from which 'no one can shrink' and was induced to think that Miss Foster had ceased to care for him. Sir Shane Leslie held a somewhat similar view, writing that a higher power intervened and sent him abroad and that he was persuaded to exchange his romance for the vocation that the Pope saw written in his face.

The facts as hitherto outlined are from Hare's narratives, as given to him by the Eton headmaster. 'Now,' said Dr Hawtrey, 'if ever you tell that story, recollect to say that it is no mere story that I have heard; it is part of my own life. Madame de Salis and her sister were my relations and I was most intimate with them. I was there when Madame de Salis made her miserable marriage. I was there when she came back terribly changed. I was there in the consultations as to whether her sister should go with her. I was with Dr and Mrs Foster when they received the letter about Count Mastai. I was there when they heard of the disappearance of the mysterious bridegroom, and I have lived to think of him as Pope Pius IX.'

Letitia returned to Ireland and on 2 December 1818 was married by the provost of Trinity College to John Henry North. Having no children of her own, she found herself *in loco parentis* to two nieces, Margaret and Mary Letitia McCreight, daughters of her sister Elizabeth, who, together with her husband, the Reverend James McCreight, died when the children were very young.

Giovanni Maria Mastai-Ferretti became Supreme Pontiff in Rome on 16 June 1846. Some time afterwards, one of Letitia's nieces was with her when a packet arrived from Rome. On opening it, Letitia exclaimed, 'Look, Giovanni Mastai!' She then showed her niece an engraving of Pio Nono in his pontifical robes, and beneath it the words, 'You made me Pope.' Their obvious meaning was that, by not marrying him, she enabled him to be ordained. The pontiff also sent to Letitia's sister a head ornament of gold and lapis lazuli, in a case with the inscription, 'Presented to Henrietta, wife of Jerome, Count de Salis, by Pope Pius IX in memory of past days'. Later on, in 1869, when he was visited by Professor Mahaffy, provost of Trinity College, and Robert Leslie of Ballybay, County Monaghan, he recalled those past days and enquired whether the Fosters still lived in those parts.

Letitia, according to a monument to her memory in Collon church, County Louth, died on 28 November 1857 in her sixtieth year, so when she met Count Mastai she would, in the words of Sydney Watson, have been at the susceptibly marriageable age of twenty-two years. Pius IX died on 7 February 1873. His pontificate is the longest in the history of the papacy. His was a tormented, turbulent and tenebrous reign. Mistaken for a liberal when he ascended the papal throne, he was instantly popular and hailed as the 'Angel Pope'. The honeymoon, however, was short-lived. In response to Curia pressure compassion was being sacrificed to the institutional Church, controversy was stifled by a litany of anathemas and the Pope struggled in vain to save the Papal States from Garibaldi. On 18 July 1870 the Vatican Council reinforced his failing secular authority by declaring him infallible. But the cannons of Victor Emmanuel were already booming over the Eternal City, Rome was now part of Italy and the new order was settling in. Pope and Curia had shut themselves up in the Vatican.

One cannot help wondering what might have been and how the Church might have progressed if only Count Giovanni Mastai-Ferretti had turned up for his appointment with Letitia Foster in the church of San Luigi de Francesci on that spring morning in 1819.

16

KING OF THE IRISH ROADS

The story of a wandering Italian boy in one of Ireland's loveliest valleys is to me one of the world's wonder stories. It makes Dick Whittington look like the prosaic English businessman that he possibly may have been.

Benedict Kiely

The story which so enthralled Ben Kiely began and ended here in Boherlahan. This wandering Italian boy was, his biographers tell us, a peddler. On his back he carried a box of prints weighing over a hundred pounds, and under that weight he would walk up to thirty miles a day. One day, when passing through our village, he espied the Moat of Ardmayle just one mile to his right. Climbing the ancient fortress, with the heavy load of pictures on his shoulders, he beheld the River Suir and, across the valley, a white mansion. Enraptured by the vision of the white house, he lay back on the grassy mound, closed his eyes and dreamt of one day living in such an abode. Awaking from his reverie, he made his way to the stately home which turned out to be Longfield House, the residence of Captain Long, who promptly ejected the intruder, threatening to set the dogs on him. But the young man knew that he would be back one day as owner, and he was, forty-two years later.

Carlo Bianconi was born at Tregolo in the Como province of Italy on 24 September 1786. His father was a farmer of good standing in the community. When Carlo was just fifteen he fell in love with Giovanna, a neighbour's daughter who had already been betrothed in her childhood to a member of the nobility. To avoid unpleasant repercussions, the father decided to apprentice him to a picture-dealer who just so happened to be leaving the district and on his way to Ireland.

Bianconi and his employer arrived in Dublin in 1802. When his eighteen months' apprenticeship came to an end, he took the money which his father had deposited for the return journey to Italy and used it to buy pictures and frames which he decided to peddle in the country. Making his way south, he arrived in Thurles, where he was set upon by would-be muggers, only to be rescued by Theobald Matthew, the future Apostle of Temperance, who remained his close friend and found him suitable lodgings in the town. In later years, when entertaining a group of priests, Bianconi recalled an amusing incident from the early days in Thurles. This account of the story is taken from the diary of the parish priest of Clonulty, Fr O'Carroll, for 1846 *[the diary is in the Diocesan Archives of Cashel and Emly]:*

> In 1804, John Hunt lodged in the same house as me in Thurles. He was then young, and a rabid bigot, eternally damning papists, though most of his friends and connections are of the same creed. Toby Matthew, now the Apostle of Temperance, was at school in Thurles at the same time. He used to be frequently in with us at our lodgings, as Hunt is his cousin germane. Well, I could not well discover at first what he meant by papists, but discovering at last its signification, I one day threw off my coat and offered to box him on the merits of the case. My challenge was accepted. We both flung off our coats and set to in good earnest, Toby acting as my bottle-holder. After some hard cuffing on both sides, I brought Hunt down at last and gave him such a thrashing

that he was never since known to use the word papist. Mr Hunt is now a respectable solicitor in Dublin.

Bianconi's robust defence of the papacy would have been due in no small measure to his relationship with Mrs Tobin, superioress of the Ursuline Convent in Thurles – an association which also began with his visits to Thurles. She put a lot of business his way by encouraging the parents of the girls, and particularly of the boarders, to buy his pictures. She also encouraged him to give up peddling and start a business, however small. But all this had a price! She questioned him regularly on his religious duties and in particular his attendance at Mass and how frequently he went to Confession. This inquisition made a lasting impression on him, because many years later, in his inaugural speech as newly elected Mayor of Clonmel, Bianconi solemnly declared, 'I am not afraid of God Almighty but I am afraid of Mrs Tobin.'

At one stage he appeared doomed to tramp on foot through life, but then, encouraged by Mrs Tobin, and even more so by Julia Bourke – a beautiful girl who reminded him of his beloved Giovanna in Italy – he finally decided to leave the roads and take on the dignity of a shopkeeper. He did this in 1806, when he set up shop as a carver and gilder in Carrick-on-Suir. Later he moved to Waterford, where he met Edmund Ignatius Rice, founder of the Christian Brothers, who encouraged him to broaden his knowledge and develop his talents through adult education. He established himself finally in Clonmel, where he rented a shop opposite the Main Guard. There he sold gilded mirrors as well as coloured prints. Some of the locals called him Brian Cooney, which was a reasonable enough shot at an alien name.

Bianconi never forgot the weary miles he had trudged tramping the Irish roads, and this experience opened his eyes to the possibilities of a cheap transport system. His opportunity came with the fall in prices of horses at the end of the Napoleonic Wars. The Battle of Waterloo was fought in June 1815; the following month Charles Bianconi launched the enterprise which was to make his name and fortune. On 6 July 1815 he started to run a one-horse car between Clonmel and Cahir. By the end of 1815 he had extended his service to link Clonmel and Limerick and had also opened a regular line from Clonmel to Thurles. The following year his car service was operating between Clonmel and Waterford and by 1819 his cars were on the road between Waterford, New Ross, Enniscorthy and Wexford. Two years later he opened a line to Cork.

By 1820 his cars were covering over 1,000 miles each day, linking the principal towns of south Leinster and east Munster. And the expansion continued. In 1857 his vehicles, locally called 'Bians', were running 4,244 miles daily in twenty counties, with cars running as far north as Letterkenny. The headquarters of this great enterprise was at Clonmel in what is now Parnell Street. Here he installed his trusted friend Daniel Hearn as his general manager. Hearn later converted the house overlooking the stable yards to Hearn's Hotel, which is still thriving today.

At a time when the British press was pouring into the ear of the world tales of marauding highwaymen on the roads of Ireland as well as tales of the supposed lawlessness, savagery and inherent dishonesty of the Irish people, Bianconi in a paper read at a British Association meeting in Dublin in 1857 had this to say:

> My conveyances, many of them carrying very important mails, have been travelling during all hours of the day and night, often in lonely and unfrequented places, and during the long period of forty-two years that my establishment has been in existence, the slightest injury has never been done by people to my property or that entrusted to my care.

As the business grew, so too did the cars. They became longer and longer, and soon four-wheeled vehicles were replacing two-wheeled ones. The four-wheeled cars were known as 'Finn McCools', after the legendary hero, whereas all his open cars continued to be known affectionately as 'Bians'. His fares were one penny farthing a mile, which may seem cheap by modern standards, but a journey of six miles in pre-Famine Ireland might cost more than a full day's wages to a labourer who earned only sixpence a day.

Bianconi showed his great business acumen and adaptability with the coming of the railways. He adapted his services to them and even invested in them. His cars became feeders to the trains. When he sold off his business in 1866, his 'Bians' were still travelling 4,000 miles of Irish roads daily, and about 900 horses were still in use.

At the age of forty he married Elizabeth, daughter of John Philpot Hayes, a prominent Dublin businessman. She was twenty years his junior. Through the Hayes family he met and formed a lasting friendship with Daniel O'Connell, who appointed him a director of the newly founded National Bank. Bianconi's son Charles Jnr was to marry Daniel O'Connell's granddaughter, and his daughter Minnie was to marry the Liberator's favourite nephew, John Coppinger O'Connell. From being a little Italian peddler of prints, Bianconi had risen to become a national institution.

But the best was still to come; the peddler's dream on the Moat of Ardmayle was about to be realised. In 1846 he purchased for £22,000 the mansion and estate of over 1,000 acres at Longfield which he had admired as a poor peddler forty-two years before. Longfield House in this parish of Boherlahan was to be his home for the remaining thirty years of his life. It was the first of his purchases of land. He was to buy a further 6,000 acres before he died. 'Money melts,' he said, 'but land holds as long as grass grows and water runs.' When he drove through the gates of Longfield House as its new owner, led by the Cashel Temperance Band resplendent in their new uniforms, the avenue was lined with his tenants, his employees and their families loudly cheering their new master. The King of the Irish Roads had finally come into his kingdom.

The year was 1846; the Great Famine had just set in. The potatoes were rotting; hunger, rents and fever were taking their toll. The population of Boherlahan parish, in which Longfield House is situated, was 7,100. In a few years it would shrink to just over 2,000. Bianconi set up soup kitchens in Longfield and got the local clergy to distribute his largesse to the poor. In 1848 Ireland had still not shaken off the effects of the Famine. Potatoes cost tenpence a stone but now Bianconi started to sell them to his tenants and employees at only fourpence a stone, and this he continued to do for the rest of his life, regardless of the market price.

Bianconi returned to his native Italy with all his family in October 1851. In contrast to his departure as a teenager, he now travelled in great style with three carriages, his own horses and a retinue of servants. During his visit, Pope Pius

IX, the great Pio Nono who appointed young Charley Bianconi as one of his honorary chamberlains, received him. His duties were to attend the papal court at certain times during the year. It was a proud moment for the Longfield family when Charley first took his place in the papal court. Bianconi was received everywhere in Italy with great acclaim as 'The Man Who Put Ireland on Wheels'.

'I remember,' he wrote to one of the younger generation, 'when I was earning a shilling a day in Clonmel, I used to live upon eightpence, and that did not prevent the people from twice making me their mayor. I did the same at Cashel and at Thurles, and that does not prevent me from at present living between the two towns on a property of seven miles circumference, or from being a JP and a DL. It gives me sincere pleasure in seeing you follow the sound principle of having your wants within your means.'

What a pity that his only son, who was so seriously in debt that he had to flee to Brussels to escape his creditors, did not follow the same sound principle. His health deteriorated in Belgium and he died at Holyhead on 2 March 1864. He was smuggled home in a large packing case disguised as a piano, because in those days bodies could be seized for debt. Then he had to be buried secretly by night in the little chapel in Boherlahan specially built by Charles Bianconi for his daughter Kate, who had died on a visit to Italy and whose remains were brought home for burial. With the fortitude of a martyr, Bianconi watched impassively as the body of young Charley was lowered into the vault to join his sister Kate and his tiny daughter Charlotte. Now there was nobody left to carry on his name.

Early in 1875 Bianconi had a stroke and lost the use of his right hand. He lingered on and died at a quarter to five on the morning of Wednesday 22 September 1875, two days before entering his ninetieth year. All night long his family and the rest of his household had kept vigil with him. As the end approached those present heard what sounded like approaching hoof beats; then came the unmistakable sounds of galloping horses on the gravel below. The grooms went rushing to the stables, only to find that none of the horses had broken loose. Yet they still heard the murmur of hoof beats, as though all the horses in Bianconi's long life had come to be with him as he set out on his last journey, this time to his true homeland.

17

Specially for Sinéad
A Wedding Homily

I knew this wasn't going to be easy and had a sense of apprehension from the moment that she broached the subject of her wedding. She came directly to the point.

'I'm getting married,' she declared. 'I want you to do the job and,' she added ominously, 'I don't want any of your canned homilies.'

'What's that supposed to mean?' I countered.

'Well, I've heard all of them. You changed your tack recently, and I like what you had to say – at first, that is – but it begins to pall after two or three airings. I want something different – a totally new presentation, if you know what I mean.'

Sinéad is a professional photographer with, I might add, a glittering array of national awards to her credit for her technical and creative expertise. When I suggested – rather cattily, I must confess – that she might like to write the homily herself and that I would consider delivering it, she brushed the gibe aside. 'I haven't got the time,' she said. 'I've got exactly ninety weddings to do before my own. That means I'll have to listen to ninety different homilies and,' she went on, now revelling in my discomfort, 'I still want mine to be different.'

'Why be difficult,' I sighed, 'when you can be impossible?'

'Oh yes, and by the way,' she continued, by way of a

parting salvo, 'there's to be no mention of photography, or of horticulture.'

'Why the ban on horticulture?' I queried.

'Because it happens to be William's occupation.'

I was about to ask if the ban on horticulture included taurine fertiliser, but she was gone, leaving me to my fate.

Inspiration came eventually from, of all unlikely sources, a bishop! And a dead one and a Protestant at that. The bishop's chessboard came to mind, and how I had used it as a visual aid when speaking about stress and how to cope with it. So I decided to adapt it to the marriage context of two young people facing into a future that was now hidden from their eyes.

What follows is basically what I said at Sinéad and William's wedding. Its inclusion in this book is intended to assist the preacher who faces the challenge of saying 'something different' at every wedding and, in the process, to sow the seeds from which his own creative thoughts will develop.

The day of the wedding arrived. After the Gospel reading I produced the chessboard, folded in two to give the appearance of a prayer-card. When I opened it and showed it to the congregation, Sinéad gave me a what's-he-up-to-now look to which I felt like responding, 'Well, you did ask for something different, and that's what you going to get.' This is what I said.

Way back at the beginning of the last millennium, there lived a man in the Persian Gulf whose name was Omar Khyyam. He was a poet and philosopher and his greatest work, *The Rubaiyat of Omar Khayyam*, is a poem in which he tries to make sense out of the enigmas of life. All around him he saw joys turning into sorrows, hopes into disappointments, successes into failures, pleasure into pain and, in the context of marriage, hands clasped together in love in the wedding ceremony becoming fists raised in anger shortly afterwards. His poem is a philosophy of reflection on these anomalies in life – a philosophy which is summed up in the lines:

'Tis all a chequerboard of Nights and Days
Where Destiny with Men for Pieces plays.

The chequerboard – the forerunner of the chessboard – was for Khayyam a microcosm of human life made up of black squares and white squares. The black squares represent suffering, death and all the ills that flesh is heir to; the white speak of the happiness and love that light up our lives when everything is right with the world.

In a few minutes Sinéad and William will pledge their lives to one another in a commitment which envisages the black and white squares of life: I take you for better (white) or for worse (black), for richer (white) or for poorer (black), in sickness (black) and in health (white), all the days of our lives. In a future now hidden from their eyes, they will move on life's chessboard with its joys (white) and sorrows (black), hopes (white) and disappointment (black), successes (white) and failures (black), pleasures (white) and pains (black), depression (black) and ecstasy (white), love (white) and hate (black), life (white) and death (black).

Today, they, and all of us, are on a white square – a square that is whiter than white – and our prayer for them is that it may always be so. But if ever you find yourselves on a black square, remember that you are touched by four white squares of deliverance. These white squares are here in this church at this very moment, and you will find help and comfort in each one of them. A word on each.

1. *The Top Square.* The Lord, the unseen but very real presence at this marriage. The Lord who beckons to you: come to me all you who labour and are overburdened and I will give you rest. The Lord who is very much a part of this ceremony. Remember that he is not just here for the day. Do not forget him once you leave this church today. Create space for him in your lives, in your home and family life. Talk to him in prayer and take your cares to him. The prayer in your booklet that you composed yourselves, pray it every day of your married life, and pray it together. Let me remind you of the words, your words: 'We thank you, Lord, for all that you have given us, our families and friends, and especially each other. We ask you to keep us faithful in our love for each other and for you. Please bless our marriage and our home and grant us a healthy family to nurture in your love. We ask this through Christ our Lord, amen.'

2. *The Squares to Left and Right.* Your parents and immediate families, to whom you owe so much – your very lives, the wholesome values of religion, love and loyalty which you have experienced in the homes that moulded you into the two lovely people that you are. Always remember all they have done for you and be truly thankful (mention could also be made here of grandparents who have two precious commodities to offer to young people: time and memories).

3. *Last of All.* Yourselves. In a few moments your two

individual lives will merge into one, symbolised by the candle. Remember that the commitment you are about to make is not a once-off thing. It may need to be renewed quite often as you go through life. Remember Paul's words: 'Do not let the sun go down on your anger'. In other words, do not go to bed on a quarrel! Recall again Paul's *Song of Love* in today's Second Reading and put it into practice in your daily lives. If you do, you won't go far wrong!

Let me finish as I began, with Omar Khayyam. Here he is addressing his sweetheart on the vicissitudes of life:

Ah Love, could thou and I with Fate conspire
To grasp this sorry scheme of things entire,
Would we not shatter it to bits – and then
Remould it nearer to the Heart's Desire!

Needless to say, I adapted this framework to my personal knowledge of Sinéad and William, and it seemed to work, because at the Sign of Peace she whispered to me, 'Ten out of ten!' Ever since, when I meet her, she assures me that she and William are still on the white squares.

By way of postscript to this chapter, the following incident from a recent wedding at which I was present is a further example of the unpredictable hazards facing the wedding homilist. The guests included a posse of punter friends of the bridegroom, who was himself actively involved in the Sport of Kings. To honour the occasion, these gentlemen took it upon themselves to open a book and hold a sweepstake on, of all things, the preacher's homily.

Bets were placed, timekeepers synchronised their watches and the result would be announced – privately, of course, out of respect for the preacher – towards the end of the wedding reception. At the dessert stage, the wagers were placed on a plate at the punters' table. It was a case of winner takes all.

Eventually Philly was declared the winner, and he was about to collect the takings when he was unexpectedly pipped at the post by the waitress who had been serving the gamblers' table. She naturally assumed that the plate, with its sizeable takings, was a gratuity in recognition of her services. She was profuse in thanking the gentlemen for their generosity as she made off with the booty, leaving the punters, and especially Philly, as also-rans!

Epilogue

Can we have hope in the future without memories, positive and negative, from the past?
Dermot A. Lane, in New Century, New Society

In retrospect, this book reads like a litany of memories 'drifting in like painted butterflies from valleys far away': memories of people, places and events that have shaped my life. Memories play a vital role in all our lives. When someone we love dies, the memories they created for us come flooding into our lives and we recreate them over and over again. How oft in graveside eulogies have I listened to the words of the poet Laurence Binyon concluding with:

At the going down of the sun and in the morning
We shall remember them.

I once heard an old soldier at the graveside of a comrade in arms, after he had recited Binyon's verses, concluding with his own poignant plea to the Creator:

Lord God of Hosts, be with us yet,
Lest we forget! Lest we forget!

That beautiful memorial prayer from the Jewish Requiem Liturgy is also often quoted:

We shall not see the familiar glowing face, the warm illuminated eyes, nor hear the beloved voice;
We shall not sit face to face across the family table or side by side in the home of a friend, or in worship;
We shall not feel the kiss that once evoked our deepest response.

Yet death has failed.

For our loved ones live and will always live through the years, not in some distant corner of our being to be uncovered only in a rare moment or by a sudden surge of recall.

They have become a presence, in-dwelling and inseparable, rooted so deep that life cannot carry us far from the cherished centre of memory and love.

Your hand, O Death, has been stayed. You cannot inflict oblivion or disappearance on those who were life of our life. They live and move within us in spheres beyond your dominion.

We thank you, O God of Life and Love, for the resurrecting gift of memory, which endows your children, fashioned in your image, with Godlike sovereign power to give immortality through love.

Blessed be thou, O God, who enable your children to remember.

The old Latin adage *Traductor traditor est* (Every translator is a traitor) ought to make every translator squirm, because when a word is translated into another language it generally loses a great deal of its meaning. One word which has lost out in the translation process is 'memory', particularly in the context of Christ's command at the Last Supper: 'Do this in memory of me.' Memory can have so many meanings. It can mean that wonderful faculty given to all of us which is capable of storing images. As we grow older some of us find it increasingly difficult to retrieve material from the storehouse of the brain. Memory can also mean the matter saved in this crammed storehouse.

But when Christ used this word at the Last Supper, he was not referring to images in the past. The Greek New Testament word for memory – 'anamnesis' – has one meaning and one meaning only: 'making present'. When this ritual act takes place at Mass – the words over the bread and wine and the separate consecration of both – then Supper and Cross are here and now made present. And we are thus able to be present to these awesome mysteries and further enabled to bring to them our own sincere sentiments of compassion, love and repentance. In this memory, we have the greatest antidote to change: God with us! Memory as making present is the kernel of the memorial prayer of the Jews, in which they thank God for the resurrecting gift of memory.

Ballinure, where I was born and raised and whose horizons extended scarcely a mile from the crossroads, now in the opening year of a new millennium finds itself at another crossroads and part of another village. It has become enveloped by the global village that is Planet Earth. The information and communications revolution has made our world a global village like never before.

Through the marvels of technology and globalisation, mushrooming satellite dishes, together with the Internet, are increasingly bombarding us with a mass culture that is alien to many of our cherished beliefs and traditions. Ireland, for better or worse, is now in the mainstream of change, and there is no issue of a global order that will not have an impact, direct or indirect, upon us. The problems of Europe and the world are becoming our problems now.

Surveys documenting the decline of the Church in the 1990s point to a number of factors: a significant fall in church attendance, particularly in urban areas; a sharp decline in vocations, leading in some instances to the closure of seminaries and religious houses; the diminishing credibility and relevance of some moral and doctrinal directives; the scandals already mentioned and, associated with these scandals, the lack of transparency in institutions. And finally, there is that bee that buzzes in bishops' bonnets: the prevalence of an unfriendly and apparently value-free media. Malcolm Muggeridge once suggested that, if the desert encounter between Christ and Satan were to take place today, there would be a fourth temptation: Christ would be offered a prime-time spot on television!

Another factor in the decline of the Church's influence is the relatively late arrival in Ireland of the Enlightenment. This process, which proclaims the primacy of reason over tradition, authority and religion, took 200 years to unfold on the continent, resulting in a thoroughly secularised Europe. It had a much shorter and easier passage in Ireland, taking just twenty years to find its roots – the two decades since the papal visit.

And what of the future? Liam Ryan suggests in his book *The Church in Politics* that, in the relationship between the Church and society in the future, the role of the Church might be that of the conscience of society. And his brother Seamus, in an on-the-ball contribution to *The Church in a New Ireland,* likens the clerical Church in Ireland to that of an overgrown, pot-bound plant which is beginning to choke itself by its own roots because they have nowhere to go. The roots of the Church are yearning to break out and to find a new ambience in which to grow, but they are too fearful to do so.

A recent UN report shows that, side by side with a rampant Celtic Tiger market economy, Ireland has the second-highest level of poverty in the industrialised world – and that for the second successive year. In a brilliant and perceptive article in *Concilium,* Leonardo Boff, the Franciscan liberation theologian, speaks of a new form of religion appearing within the very market itself. He describes this new religion as the religion of commodities, a religion which promises happiness, life and meaning in this world. The fundamental dogma of the religion of commodities is this: money is all-powerful; money is what gets things done. Advertising fulfils the function of evangelisation, which proclaims the good news of salvation. 'Happy' and 'successful' people are real sacraments, in that they are filled with energy and life. The temples of this religion are the banks, the priests are the bankers and financiers and, like ourselves, they too occasionally fall from grace. The places of pilgrimage are the shopping malls, especially the ones that open on the day of the Lord! This is yet another instance of secularism and consumerism pushing God into ever-shrinking corners of our lives.

The 'God question' – putting God the Unchanged and Unchangeable first – must be the top priority for all of us as we enter the portals of the new millennium. Prophets of doom have been warning us of dark times ahead. I feel that we may all find a message of encouragement in the story of a man who had a dream of standing at the gate of the year 2000. To the angel guarding the entrance he said: 'Give me a light so that I may walk safely through this place'.

The angel replied: 'Do not be afraid of the dark; go out into it and put your hand into the hand of God. That shall stand to you as a light in the darkness.'

Did he not also say: 'Even though I walk through the valley of the shadow of death, I fear no evil; for thou art with me; thy rod and thy staff, they comfort me' (Psalm 23:4).

More Interesting Books

My Village
My World

John M. Feehan

This is a book that never palls or drags. It is boisterous and ribald and I am tempted to say that it is by far the funniest book I have ever read. It is also an accurate and revealing history of rural Ireland half a century ago and more. John M. Feehan writes beautifully throughout. I love this book.

From the Foreword by John B. Keane

My Village – My World is a fascinating account of ordinary people in the countryside. It depicts a way of life that took thousands of years to evolve and mature and was destroyed in a single generation. As John M. Feehan says 'Nobody famous ever came from our village. None of its inhabitants ever achieved great public acclaim ... The people of our village could be described in government statistics as unskilled. That would be a false description. They were all highly skilled, whether in constructing privies or making coffins, digging drains or cutting hedges, droving cattle or tending to stallions ... I do not want to paint a picture of an idyllic village like Goldsmith's phony one. We had our sinners as well as our saints ...'

Preaching in Stories

James A. Feehan

Preaching in Stories is a plea for creative preaching, a return to the storytelling process in breaking the bread of God's word. Drawing on almost four decades of preaching Fr Feehan builds his case on the interaction of three stories in the Sunday homily – the story or faith experience of the preacher, the story of God and the story of the listeners. As well as stories galore there are some fine examples of creative writing as in the story of the Four Friends where the author sees the miracle of the healing of the paralysed man through the eyes of four different people, pictured in his imagination as the four friends who let the sick man down through the roof.

Stories for Preachers

James A. Feehan

Stories for Preachers is written from a conviction that the massive boredom in our churches today stems from the fact that the average Sunday worshipper is incapable of sustained listening for more than a few minutes. If it can't be said in six to seven minutes it can't be got across at all. The short homily calls for long and painstaking preparation and needs to be illuminated by apt and imaginative illustrations.

The preacher today is faced with the challenge of bringing the reality of Christ to a people bewildered by the fantasies of the media – and *Stories for Preachers* is an attempt to meet this challenge.